IN THEIR OWN WORDS

Practices of Quotation in Early Medieval History-Writing

In Their Own Words

*Practices of Quotation in Early
Medieval History-Writing*

JEANETTE BEER

UNIVERSITY OF TORONTO PRESS
Toronto Buffalo London

© University of Toronto Press 2014
Toronto Buffalo London
www.utppublishing.com
Printed in Canada

ISBN 978-1-4426-4754-1

Library and Archives Canada Cataloguing in Publication

Beer, Jeanette M. A., author
In their own words : practices of quotation in early medieval history-writing / Jeanette Beer.

Includes bibliographical references.
ISBN 978-1-4426-4754-1 (bound)

1. Middle Ages – Historiography.   2. Quotations – History – Middle
Ages, 500–1500.   3. French literature – To 1500 – Criticism, Textual.
4. Literature, Medieval – Criticism, Textual.   5. Civilization, Medieval,
in literature.   I. Title.

D116.B43 2014   808.06'69091   C2013-908068-6

University of Toronto Press acknowledges the financial assistance to its
publishing program of the Canada Council for the Arts and the Ontario
Arts Council.

University of Toronto Press acknowledges the financial support of
the Government of Canada through the Canada Book Fund for its
publishing activities.

For Olivia, Miranda, Fiona, and Juliet

Contents

Foreword

This is a book about quotation in early medieval history-writing, a subject that would appear at first sight unproblematic were it not for constantly evolving assumptions about the nature and role not only of quotation but of history itself. For centuries, history was an important branch of literature rather than distinct from it, but in the nineteenth century it became a discipline apart in which it became conventional to identify truth with fact, while fiction was opposed to truth. Positivism no longer reigns, but oppositionally defined systems continue to flourish, and this, coupled with the sheer enormity of the medieval historiographical corpus, makes writing about it such a challenge that the recent *Cambridge Companion to Medieval French Literature* omits it entirely.[1]

The ambiguity of the word "historia," signifying both history and story, symbolizes the unusual complexity of medieval historiography in all its hybridity and fluidity. Generic margins blurred into one another, and for many centuries hagiographical works and *chansons de geste* served, practically speaking, as history. The works selected for analysis here, however, are in prose; they date from the ninth to the thirteenth century; all are major historiographical works; and each is the first extant example of a particular type of history-writing. This primacy gives them the appearance of having appeared *ex nihilo*, but the reality must have been otherwise. At the nexus of Latin and vernacular traditions, they are the inheritors of both, and it is their quotation practices that will provide a window upon the relationship between inherited classical and contemporary vernacular influences as they intersected in the early centuries of the Middle Ages, a formative period of history-writing in the west.

The first work, Nithard's *Historiae de dissensionibus filiorum Ludovici Pii*,[2] is extraordinary for its quotation of two sets of vernacular oaths, which are embedded in its third book. These oaths, "The Strasbourg Oaths," are the first extant piece of French, and are an exciting gift to linguists, who have been happily discussing their significance for decades. They are rarely discussed within their *literary* context because their content is so boringly conventional to literary scholars. To modern historians also the oaths appear unremarkable, since the inclusion of documents *is* unremarkable in a modern history. But Nithard's practices of quotation were iconoclastic in the ninth century.

The *Gesta Francorum*, which appeared anonymously soon after the Battle of Ascalon (12 August 1099),[3] is the first eyewitness account of the First Crusade, composed by a follower of Bohemond from the Norman duchy of Apulia. Criticized by a supercilious churchman as a "rustic little book put together by I don't know who,"[4] it became a favoured source for later histories of the First Crusade. The unpretentious style of the *Gesta* lasted well, but misunderstanding of its quotation practices has led to anachronistic judgments even by its otherwise excellent nineteenth-century editor, the eminent historian Louis Bréhier. Bréhier was convinced that the text's anonymous author was by nature terse and factual, a modern historian *avant la lettre* who could not conceivably have written certain parts of the *Gesta Francorum*. Bréhier's anachronistic expectations, historical or otherwise, have dangerous consequences, as will become evident in our analysis of the *Gesta*'s quotation practices.

La Conquête de Constantinople,[5] written in the early thirteenth century by Geoffrey of Villehardouin, marshal of Champagne and Romania and a prime negotiator in the Fourth Crusade, is the first French prose history extant. Villehardouin guarantees the truth of his narrative on the grounds that it has been written by "cil qui a toz les conseils fu" (one who was present at all the councils). He claims also that he never knowingly lied ("ainc n'i menti de mot a son escient") (an interesting variant on the truth claim, not to lie being not necessarily the equivalent of telling the truth!). Paradoxically, it is Villehardouin's very participation in all the councils that now makes his reports of the leaders' negotiations suspect to some modern historians, but there is no question that, like the author of the *Gesta*, he was overawed by the magnitude of the Crusading enterprise. Sadly for him, the enterprise ultimately failed and he was unable, like twentieth-century war historians, to declare that "never in the field of human conflict was so much owed by so many to so few." After commenting early in the work on the overwhelming odds facing the Crusaders at Constantinople ("Et mult estoient peril-lousement, que onques par tant poi de gent ne furent assegié tant de gent en nulle ville" [And they were in dire straits, for never were so many besieged in any city by so few), the last part of the chronicle records his constant attempts to salvage the Fourth Crusade's succession of failures.

Not surprisingly, the literary allusions that colour his narration of the military struggles of an ever-dwindling remnant of Crusading leaders are Rolandian, but apart from the vernacular epic, his literary allusions are of the most general sort. Biblical references and proverbial wisdom play the largest role. The conciseness of his narration gives us an impression of truthful simplicity, but an examination of his quotation practices reveals a more complex picture. Analysis of his quotation practices – for example, his self-referencing, his citation of "the book," and his selective use of oral techniques – demonstrate that his history is multivoiced and highly sophisticated. Of crucial importance also in this intensely personal record are the words he presents – and does not present – as direct speech. If ever *argumentum e silentio* is justified, it is in Villehardouin's *La Conquête de Constantinople*, where the author's silences are as telling as the words in which he "never lied."

Robert de Clari's *La Conquête de Constantinople*[6] was composed around the same time and in the middle of the same event, but by an eyewitness participant whose cultural and professional background differed markedly from Villehardouin's. Robert knew nothing of the inner workings of the councils, and is noticeably unreliable on dates, figures, or on any event outside his personal experience, although he accurately reflects the preoccupations and language of the class of *povres chevaliers* to which he belongs. His history is the perfect foil to Villehardouin's dignified and terse account. The similarities and the differences in their quotation practices provide significant information not only about the Fourth Crusade but also about the traditions that were being forged in early vernacular history-writing.

Li Fet des Romains,[7] compiled and translated from all the classical texts on Julius Caesar that were known to the thirteenth century, is the first work of ancient historiography and the first biography[8] to appear in French, thus pioneering a long line of foundational and formative narratives devoted to "that quasi-mythic protagonist in the development of Western culture."[9] This new venture in vernacular history-writing differs from our first four histories in that its narrator has not participated in the events of his narrative, his sources are literary sources, and he is translating their Latin words into a Romance vernacular, quotation at one remove.

Latin compilation was not, of course, new.[10] From St. Augustine onwards, the *speculum* offered a mirror of good conduct for the improvement of its readers. In the twelfth century, *flores historiarum, flores chronicorum,* and *flores temporum* offered selections of edifying material culled from the past. *Li Fet des Romains* is different in kind from these compilations, however, for the historical interest of Caesar's career is the dominant factor for the translator as he systematically assembles the disparate parts of the Caesarean corpus into a coherent whole. Composed by someone who is familiar with rhetorical tradition – even *in medias res* he discusses questions of authority – it yields important information about medieval attitudes to the *auctores*. The translator-compiler's magisterial comments on the nature of the source material, its proper handling, and its translation make *Li Fet des Romains* an invaluable commentary on the relationship that obtained between classical and medieval practices of quotation in history-writing.

An important preliminary to the examination of this wide-ranging selection of histories during the formative period of Western history-writing is to outline their inherited assumptions about history, since history-writing flowed into the Middle Ages from antiquity with something of an undertow, as John O. Ward nicely expresses it. Toward the end of his life St. Augustine even deemed it an essentially invalid activity![11]

Isidore of Seville, the prism through whom antiquity's practices were refracted for many centuries, is here a helpful guide.[12] According to Isidore, history, which records what deserves to be remembered ("quidquid memoria dignum est"), is the narration of events. It is named "history" "apo tou historein," (ἀπὸ τοῦ ἱστορεῖν), which Isidore (incorrectly) translates as seeing ("videre") and learning ("cognoscere"). Eyewitness accounts of events are the best source of information and the best guarantee of historical truth, for what is seen is related without lies: "quae enim videntur, sine mendacio proferuntur." History serves as a didactic lesson for humanity, and for this purpose even pagan history is useful. The "res verae" (true things) of antiquity can be sifted by the moderns for the purpose of demonstrating truth ("veritas"), which separates history ("res verae quae factae sunt" – true things that actually happened) from fable ("fabulae vero sunt quae nec factae sunt nec fieri possunt" – but fables are what never happened and could never happen).

Isidore's etymology of "verus" is informative by its very lack of information: "verus, a veritate; hinc et verax. Maior est veritas quam verus, quia non veritas a vero, sed verus a veritate descendit" (true, from truth; hence also truthful. Truth is greater than true, because truth does not descend from true, but true descends from truth).[13] Truth, being truth, and thus presumably distinguishable from falsehood, needs definition merely by an etymology, not by its properties, and Isidore posits for it a hierarchy of values by word-class in which "true" is subordinated to "truth" because the adjective "verus" derives from, and is chronologically subordinate to, the substantive "veritas." Such theorizing has metaphysical implications. Truth and fact can be polarized, with preference for the former over the latter in contexts of apparent conflict. I have examined elsewhere[14] the paradoxical developments that ensued from these medieval presumptions about truth, and the complex literary tradition of these truth assertions. Isidorean tenets were an important backdrop for that book, as they are here.

All the works treated are based upon the belief, implicit and often explicit, that history is different from fable in that it deals with truth (however defined!) and – an important concomitant – that its truth is best guaranteed by someone who has experienced it personally. Nithard makes reference to his own participation in the battle of Fontenoy, after which, disillusioned, he plods on with the "disagreeable task" of chronicling his royal family's disputes only because he fears that someone less informed might presume to record events differently from the way they actually happened. The unpretentious author of the *Gesta* claims that although no one, whether cleric or layman, could possibly narrate the totality of all that happened, he will contribute his "little bit," aware of the value of his eyewitness record of the event of a lifetime. Villehardouin validates his narrative of the conquest of Constantinople by his personal experiences as diplomat, negotiator, soldier, and administrator in the Fourth Crusade, and claims that he "never, to the best of his knowledge, spoke an untrue word." A true account of the conquest of Constantinople was recorded also by Robert of Clari "who was there and saw it." Even *Li Fet des Romains* in its translation of Caesarean material reflects the same Isidorean assumptions about truth and eyewitness history. Believing that the truthful narration of *res gestae* is best guaranteed by eyewitness experience but unaware that Caesar was the author of *Bellum gallicum*, the compiler of *Li Fet des Romains* invents eyewitness status for "Julius Celsus Constantinus" to reinforce "Celsus's" authority.

Thus Isidore's definition of history is a useful starting point[15] in these early medieval centuries at the confluence of classical and vernacular traditions when the hybridity of medieval works and "the incontrovertible orality of medieval culture"[16] blur generic margins. Although only one of our historical texts is close enough to the academic traditions of antiquity to be called "academic discourse,"[17] and although the provenance and *raison d'être* of the works in this book are various, all illustrate the way in which inherited traditions melded with vernacular traditions to create new modes of history-writing.

Examination of the quotation practices of these works at the interstices of past and present is of particular interest since it provides a window upon a complex subject. The various features that will be included under this rubric are *ipsissima verba* (actual words verifiably uttered), *oratio recta* (direct speech/direct discourse), and *oratio obliqua* (indirect speech/indirect discourse, including free indirect speech/free indirect discourse),[18] literary quotation, allusion, translation, citation of sources, and self-referencing. Analysis of these features reveals how similar their assumptions were about practices inherited from antiquity and how similar their adaptations were to a new medieval age. It reveals also the very real discrepancies that exist between medieval and modern usage. It is only when these discrepancies are uncovered that we shall properly understand the nature of medieval history-writing itself.

Acknowledgments

During the writing of this book, I have been helped by many people. As a member of the Senior Common Room at Lady Margaret Hall, Oxford, where I did an undergraduate degree many years ago, and as a senior member also of St. Hilda's College, Oxford, which has granted me various visitorships and fellowships over the years, I have profited greatly from the scholarly conversation and collegiality of the fellows at those two colleges. Invaluable help has also come from All Souls College through the kind offices of the manciple, Paul Gardner. By allowing me to return to one of its residences every term, All Souls College facilitates my transatlantic commute, which would not otherwise have been possible. I am grateful also to my American alma mater, Columbia University, where I have been an Associate of the Medieval Seminar since 1972. Material for this book was presented to that seminar on two occasions, and the discussions of my medieval colleagues were invaluable, as were bibliographical suggestions for Chapter 2 from two other seminar associates, Robert Somerville and Louis Hamilton. I wish here also to express my appreciation to the Schoff Fund at the University Seminars at Columbia University for their help in the publication of this book.

Three libraries have provided crucial assistance at every stage of my work, and I owe much to the services of the reference staff at the Bodleian Library, Oxford, the staff of the Taylor Institution, Oxford, and, on the other side of the Atlantic, to Ann Watkins, Reference/Circulation Librarian at the John Cotton Dana Library, Rutgers University, Newark. Finally, I want to thank my husband Colin for his continuing encouragement and support. *Sine qua non.*

IN THEIR OWN WORDS

Practices of Quotation in Early Medieval History-Writing

Chapter One

The First Words of French

Nithard's *Historiae de dissensionibus filiorum Ludovici Pii*

The first piece of recorded French is a quotation. It occurs in the third book of Nithard's *Historiae de dissensionibus filiorum Ludovici Pii*, and records two sets of vernacular oaths sworn at Strasbourg by the royal brothers Louis the German and Charles the Bald when they allied themselves in AD 842 against their older brother Lothar. Such a quotation would not be unusual in a modern history. In its own time, however, it was unprecedented, even iconoclastic. Not only were "the Strasbourg Oaths"[1] *ipsissima verba*, the actual words uttered by the parties who met at Strasbourg (then called Argentaria) on 14 February 842. They were also *ipsissima verba* in two barbarous (i.e., non-Latin) languages: the so-called "lingua teudisca" (German) and the "lingua romana" (French). Why did Nithard resort to such an unusual tactic in his *Histories*?

Modern explanations range widely and, more often than not, are anachronistic. Some see Nithard's inclusion of the oaths as a function of his respect for the document; others see it as exhilarated popularism or enthusiastic endorsement of the vernacular. "The Strasbourg Oaths" have even been described as a "monument affirming the use of the French popular language … and the progressive emancipation of the French language."[2] The best way to assess them is to examine them in their original context. Nithard wrote his *Histories* as a command performance at the request of his young cousin and overlord Charles II (Charles the Bald). Charles asked him to record the events of their time for posterity because of the "persecution" of Charles and his brother Louis by their older brother Lothar.

The task appears simple, but the manner in which Nithard carries it out is unusual. Nithard's own explanations of intent are crucial. At the beginning of the work, addressing his remarks to Charles, he notes that in May 841, before they entered Châlons-sur-Marne about a month prior to the battle of Fontenoy, Charles asked Nithard to record the events. Nithard says he would have found the task agreeable, "placida res" (a placid thing), if only he had had the leisure for it. Unfortunately, he could work at it only sporadically, and he apologizes for any resulting omissions or neglected details. He speaks respectfully to Charles, calling him "mi domine" (my lord). But there is no obsequiousness here, or anywhere in the *Histories*. Nithard is, after all, a member of the royal household in his own right.[3]

Moving to the specifics of the task, Nithard reveals that, when beginning his narration of the dissensions among Louis's sons, he had intended to make no mention of Louis, "pii patris vestri" (your pious father). He realized, however, that the dissensions had their roots in the events of Louis's reign, and the truth of the family's disputes would have been obscured by the omission. Also, if he omitted Louis, he would have to omit Charles's "genuinely venerable ancestor" Charlemagne. That crucial comment reveals the imperial model against whom Nithard compares the present royal family.

Speaking to Charles again in the prologue to the second book, he says that, having traced the origins of the dissensions, he will attempt to outline for the curious reader the reasons for Lothar's continuing "persecution" of his brothers. By this clear definition and delimitation of his subject, Nithard abjures any annalistic intent in favour of the more restricted task of exposing Lothar and justifying the alliance of Louis and Charles after their father's death. Pleading weakness after the difficulties he has endured, he again asks Charles's indulgence for any relevant detail he may have overlooked. Book two ends in an upbeat fashion after the rout of Lothar's troops at the battle of Fontenoy, at which battle, he says, he made a significant contribution to the combatants: "quibus haud modicum supplementum Domino auxiliante prebui" (to whom I furnished no small assistance with God's help, p. 78).

At the beginning of the third book, a switch in tone is obvious. Nithard addresses his readers rather than Charles, stating that the task of writing the *Histories* has become disagreeable – the very antithesis of "a placid thing."[4] He explains that he feels shame when anyone says anything evil about "our family," and therefore it is especially distasteful to have to say it himself: "Quoniam sinistrum me quiddam ex genere nostro ut audiam pudet, referre praesertim quam maxime piget" (Since it shames me to hear anything bad originating from our family, it is most especially painful for me to report it, p. 78). With that ominous sentence, he begins the book in which "The Strasbourg Oaths" are embedded, explaining that he would have liked to terminate the *Histories* with the battle of Fontenoy. Only his desire to prevent events from being misrepresented by less scrupulous informants causes him to continue the task he has been set.

In the fourth and final prologue, Nithard states even more strongly that his troubled mind ("mens anxia") would like an "out" not only from the *Histories*, but also from the disputes themselves. Unfortunately, he is destined to be swept along willy-nilly in the powerful squalls ("validis procellis"). He can neither escape from politics nor hope to influence the events themselves. All he can do is record the truth and hope for posterity's sake that he can prevent unwanted error.

Along with his four prologues, the opening section of the *Histories* – a eulogy of Charlemagne – is crucial to understanding the work. It provides the *exemplum* by which the family is to be judged – and found wanting. Good flowed from the memory of Charlemagne: he was "bone memoriae" (of good memory); his old age was good, "in senectute bona decedens" (dying in good old age); and he left Europe replete with all goodness ("omni bonitate repletam reliquit"). *That* Charles deserved to be called "magnus": "merito magnus imperator ab universis nationibus vocatus" (deservedly called great emperor by all nations). He was a real man, a "vir." Combining total wisdom and total virtue, he was head and shoulders above everyone in his time: "omni sapientia et omni virtute humanum genus suo in tempore adeo praecellens ut omnibus orbem inhabitantibus terribilis" (in his time so superior in all wisdom and in all virtue to the human race that he was terrible to all the inhabitants of the earth). Terrible but also lovable ("amabilis") and admirable ("admirabilis"). This made his whole reign honest and useful in all ways: "per hoc omne imperium omnibus modis, ut cunctis manifeste claruit, honestum et utile effecit" (because of this he made all his reign honest and useful in all ways, as was brilliantly apparent to everyone).

Among the superb qualities exhibited by this paragon of perfection, one is singled out specifically by Nithard: Charlemagne's success in taming the Franks and the barbarians so that they never dared to make open attacks on the empire. He writes, "Nam super omne quod ammirabile fateor fore, Francorum barbarorumque ferocia ac ferrea corda, que nec Romana potentia domare valuit, hic solus moderato terrore ... repressit" (For above everything that I consider to be admirable, he alone, with a healthy dose of terror, reigned in the fierce, ferocious hearts of the Franks and the barbarians, whom Roman power had not been strong enough to tame). His thirty-two-year reign was a perfectly happy one, as were the fourteen years of his imperial reign: "Regnavit feliciter per annos duos et XXX imperiique gubernacula nihilominus cum omni felicitate per annos quatuordecim possedit" (He reigned felicitously throughout thirty-two years and manned the controls of the empire similarly with all felicity for a full fourteen years). Here was a model to be emulated! Charlemagne's imperial majesty is the contrastive backdrop against which his less than majestic descendants squander their imperial heritage in petty squabbling, and every epithet used in this opening paragraph to describe Charlemagne is an indirect swipe at later members of the royal family.

The mannered rhetoric of Nithard's carefully constructed panegyric of Charlemagne with its repetitions, alliterations, paradoxes, and plays on sound and sense was an elegant contribution to the legend which in the eighth century had been building around Charlemagne.[5] In the *Histories,* however, its prime function is to contrast Charlemagne's universality, goodness, and felicity with the absence of those qualities in Charlemagne's successors during their *less than felicitous* reigns. The bathos of the transition from Nithard's opening paragraph eulogizing Charlemagne to the narrative proper is unmistakable: "Heres autem tante sublimitatis, Lodhuwicus" (The heir to such sublimity, Louis, p. 4).

Nithard now begins his narrative of the troubles. He sets the scene with his characterization of an undoubtedly pious king who is a less than dynamic heir of Charlemagne's imperium. Louis, fearing ("metuens," p. 8) his three brothers, has them tonsured. The anxious father ("anxius pater," p. 8) is concerned for the future of the newborn Charles; he revises his plans for the partition of the empire, pleads with the other sons on Charles's behalf, and persuades his first-born Lothar to agree that a portion of the empire may be given to Charles. Lothar will become Charles's tutor and defender against all enemies. Lothar confirms his consent with an oath: "Lodharius consensit ac sacramento testatus est" (p. 8).

Understandably, Lothar regrets his compliance almost immediately. He twice deposes his father, and even imprisons Louis and the young Charles for a time. Lothar clearly is the villain of the *Histories,* an important role for Nithard to establish for him, since by primogeniture Lothar's expectations of empire were legitimate. They were even supported briefly by Pope Gregory IV who, however, quickly repented, having been seized by remorse ("penitudine correptus," p. 16), says

Nithard with divine omniscience – and quickly returned to Rome. When Lothar eventually submits to his father (at Worms, 30 May 839), Nithard dramatizes Lothar's transgressions by casting him as the Prodigal Son, sacramentalizing the occasion with a rare[6] use of direct speech that incorporates a quotation from the Bible. Lothar confesses his sins in an expanded version of Luke 15:18's "Father I have sinned against heaven and before thee" – "Pater, peccavi in caelum et coram te." His confession is worded as: "Novi me coram Deo et te, domine pater, deliquisse; non regnum sed indulgentiam et ut gratiam tuam merear quęso" (I recognize, my lord and father, that I have failed God and you; I seek not the empire but your indulgence, and that I may merit your forgiveness, p. 30).

Louis's generous forgiveness of Lothar and Lothar's public acceptance of his father's terms for the division of the empire are then presented in a second piece of direct speech: "Ecce, fili, ut promiseram, regnum omne coram te est: divide illud, prout libuerit. Quod si tu diviseris, parcium electio Karoli erit; si autem nos illud diviserimus, similiter parcium electio tua erit" (Here, my son, is the whole empire in front of you, as I had promised; divide it up as you please. But if you divide it, Charles will choose the parts; if, however, we divide it, the choice of the parts will be yours, p. 30). This deal, highlighted by Nithard's presentation of it in direct speech and its quasi-Biblical status, becomes a keystone pledge to which Nithard reverts several times in the *Histories* (pp. 28, 40, 52, 92, 118). It is Lothar's breach of this solemn promise, argues Nithard, that makes the eventual alliance of Louis the German and Charles the Bald against their older brother a moral imperative.

With the exception of this speech, Nithard employs third-person reporting for pledging, which constitutes a leitmotiv of the first two books. By choosing to narrate "the troubles" through a seemingly endless string of promises, Nithard exposes the bewildering complexity – and tedium – of political alliances before Fontenoy. The *Histories* might well have been called *Historiae de sacramentis et coniurationibus filiorum Ludovici pii* (*Histories of the oaths and mutual swearings of the sons of Louis the Pious*) instead of *Historiae de dissensionibus filiorum Ludovici pii* (*Histories of the dissensions of the sons of Louis the Pious*)! It should be noted in passing that Nithard's concentration upon this aspect of the years before Fontenoy reveals his lucid awareness of the territorial issues that motivated the three sons in their endless promises of good faith and commitment. Janet Nelson even surmises that territorial issues were responsible for Nithard's disillusionment in book three.[7] A summary of the occurrences of "sacramentum" (oath), "jurare" (swear), and "jurejurandum" (swearing), thus arbitrarily excluding the lesser "convenire" (come to an agreement), "fides" (promise, guarantee), "foedus" (treaty), "pactio" (pact), "placitum" (agreement), "promittere" (promise), and "testari" (declare), follows.

Here is *coniuratio ad nauseam*: In 834, Charles's mother Judith takes advantage of Lothar's withdrawal and her husband's return to power to return from Lombardy to Aix, where she is obliged, together with her household, to swear an oath that she did not commit the crimes of which she was accused (p. 20).[8] Lothar, having captured Châlon, exacts an oath of allegiance from Guérin in return for his life (p. 22). Lothar swears to his father never again to cross into "France" unless by Louis's order, and never again to stir up trouble in the empire (p. 24). Hilduin, abbot of St. Denis, Gérard, count of Paris, and the inhabitants of those regions swear an oath of allegiance to Charles (p. 26). Louis gifts a section of the empire between the Seine and the Loire to Charles, and sends Charles there to receive an oath of allegiance (p. 26). Lothar is informed that if he respects his father's wishes concerning Charles, the empire – minus Bavaria – will be divided between him and Charles. Both sides agree and swear to bring it about (p. 30). Louis and Lothar meet the next day to work out the details of the agreement they have just sworn (p. 30). Three days later Lothar, through his envoys, asks his father to proceed with the division of the empire, and renounces the option to do it himself. They testify by their sworn faith that Lothar is deferring his choice only through ignorance of the territories concerned (p. 32).

Louis sends Lothar to Italy, reminding him of the many oaths he has sworn, the many revolts he has led, and the many times he has been pardoned (p. 32). He orders the inhabitants of the kingdom of Aquitaine to swear allegiance to Charles, which they do (p. 34). Louis dies and Lothar moves immediately to his promised territories, ordering anyone whose loyalty is dubious to take an oath of fidelity (p. 38). Lothar then enters Charles's territory, and Hilduin, abbot of St. Denis, and Gérard, count of Paris, switch sides. Seeing this, Pippin, son of Bernard king of the Lombards, and some others renege on an oath of allegiance they had sworn to Charles (p. 44). Charles's leaders consent to a truce with Lothar, provided that the latter henceforth be Charles's "fidus amicus" (faithful friend), as befits brothers, and that he not initiate hostilities against his brother Louis; otherwise, the oath they have sworn could become null and void. By this means they rescue their king from danger and free themselves from the oath they have sworn. Even before the envoys who had sworn to these things have dispersed, Lothar attempts to subvert several of them (p. 48).

Bernard of Septimania abstains from allying himself with Charles, saying that he has already sworn an oath to Pippin that neither will enter into any pact without the consent of the other (p. 50). He promises to try to return with them. If he cannot, he promises to release himself from his oath to Pippin and to them, and to try to return in 15 days (p. 50). (He does neither.) Nomenoë, ruler of the Bretons, swears fidelity to Charles (p. 52). Charles makes his way to Paris and promises pardon to all who submit, expulsion to all who refuse. Those unwilling to submit flee when they see a merchant fleet arriving, unexpectedly displaying the cross on which the deserters had sworn fidelity to Charles (p. 56).

Lothar receives defectors from among Louis's supporters and returns to Bavaria, leaving Duke Adalbert of Metz to receive the oath of fidelity from the inhabitants there (p. 60). Envoys from Lothar complain that Charles has ventured beyond agreed boundaries. Charles replies through envoys that he has done so only because he has been assured of no security in the territories that Lothar has guaranteed to him under oath (p. 62). Louis and Charles send a message to Lothar, guaranteeing his safety under oath if he will surrender to them (p. 70). Louis and Charles make further overtures to Lothar (on 21 June 841). Through envoys, Lothar swears his only reason for delaying is his desire for the common good (p. 74). Louis and Charles trust in this oath (p. 74), and since a truce has been confirmed by oath, they return to their camp (p. 74). Lothar's envoys convey his demands and his claims to the empire, but make no response to the overtures of Louis and Charles. Louis and Charles meet on 25 June 841 to fight Lothar's army as they had sworn they would (p. 76).

The time is almost ripe for Strasbourg because the defeat Lothar suffers at Fontenoy is not decisive enough to deter him. In September 841, Bishop Emmo, on Charles's behalf, urges Lothar to be mindful of his promises to his father and remember God's judgment against him. Lothar should cease his persecution of God's holy church, take pity on widows and orphans, and stop his inroads into Charles's territory to prevent a second internecine struggle of the Christian people (p. 92). Lothar then tries to make peace with Charles, "thinking by a ruse," writes Nithard, "to deceive both brothers," but Charles responds that he will not violate the treaty he has sworn with Louis on the grounds that it does not seem fitting to abandon to Lothar the kingdom his father bestowed on him "a Mosa usque Sequanum" (from Meuse to

Seine, p. 94). Several months of uncertainties reach a climax when Louis and Charles meet at Argentaria (Strasbourg) and deliver two speeches, Louis in German and Charles in French. They then swear "the Strasbourg Oaths."

Although the preliminary speeches were delivered as two separate speeches in two different languages, they are presented not as *ipsissima verba* (the actual words spoken) but as one long Latin paraphrase, the rhetorical nature of which is marked by the adverb "*sic*" (they spoke in words like this, or to this effect). This speech conforms, therefore, to the conventional practice of Latin historiography, and Nithard allowed the vernacular originals of it to suffer the customary fate of all vernacular documents, *viz.*, oblivion. There were valid reasons. This was conventional procedure in a history; the redaction of two formal speeches in the vernacular would have been rebarbative to readers; the speech is the culminating moment of the task Nithard took on, namely an important justification for posterity of the brothers' alliance against their older brother, lest another, misguided party – "quilibet, quocumque deceptus" (someone or other who has somehow been misled, p. 80) – try to launch an alternative version of events.

From the outset, the speech enlists the listener in the brothers' grievance, appealing directly to all present: "Quotiens Lodharius me et hunc fratrem meum, post obitum patris nostri, insectando usque ad internecionem delere conatus sit nostis" (You know how many times after our father's death Lothar has tried to destroy me and my brother by pursuing us to the point of utter destruction, p. 102). Familiar themes of fraternity, Christendom, the Christian people, the common good, and God's justice are again invoked. Lothar's continuing persecution is stressed, and his crimes listed. Then, because they believe that some of those present may doubt their good faith and the firmness of their commitment, the brothers say they have decided to swear their commitment to each other in the presence of their retainers.

This speech of persuasion prepares for the culminating act: the swearing. The text of the French oath as pledged by Louis is:

Pro Deo amur et pro christian poblo et nostro commun salvament, d'ist di in avant, in quant Deus savir et podir me dunat, si salvarai eo cist meon fradre Karlo et in adjudha et in cadhuna cosa, si cum om per dreit son fradra salvar dift, in o quid il mi altresi fazet et ab Ludher nul plaid nunquam prindrai, qui, meon vol, cist meon fradre Karle in damno sit. (p. 104)[9]

(For the love of God and for the Christian people and our common salvation, from this day forward, insofar as God grants me the knowledge and power, I shall succour this my brother Charles both in aid and in everything, as a brother rightly should succour his brother, inasmuch as he does likewise for me and I shall never enter into any agreement with Lothar which with my consent may be harmful to this my brother Charles.)

The French army of Charles the Bald pledges its loyalty as follows:

Si Lodhuuigs sagrament quę son fradre Karlo jurat, conservat, et Karlus meos sendra de suo part non lostanit, si io returnar non l'int pois, ne io ne neuls cui eo returnar int pois, in nulla ajudha contra Lodhuwig nun li iv er. (pp. 106–8)

(If Louis keeps the oath that he swore to his brother Charles and Charles, my lord, does not for his part keep it, if I cannot deter him from it, neither I, nor anyone I can deter from it, will be of any help to him against Louis.)

The same pledges are then presented in German.

The modern reader will find these oaths unremarkable. And in the ninth century they *were* unremarkable, the result of a fairly standard set of procedures in the chancery that Nithard had no need to outline for his contemporaries. The preparation process involved several stages.[10] An initial draft of the documents would be compiled in Latin, and the desired content would be couched in carefully chosen phrases from a chancery formulary. When the composite of relevant formulae was completed, the overall content of the drafted documents would require approval not only within the chancery but also from the royal leaders or their political representatives. Then the Latin text would be translated into French and German by scribes of the royal chancery. It has been surmised that Nithard himself, being trilingual, may have had charge of the translation.[11] Since he had chancery access at all times, he might have assumed that responsibility if he attributed extraordinary importance to an otherwise routine interlingual transference. This was, however, translation of the most prosaic sort, involving (indeed, demanding!) a *verbum pro verbo* (word for word) approach. It is more likely, therefore, that any input from a member of the royal family, especially one who was its official diplomat and historian, would have come after the initial stages of translation.

"The Strasbourg Oaths" differ only slightly from *sacramenta firmitatis* (solemn oaths) or *sacramenta fidelitatis* (oaths of fidelity), having been sworn by brothers and having encouraged the defection of retainers under certain circumstances. The situation required no formulaic innovations. Louis's oath to Charles comprises:

a) The areas of pertinence – persons served by the agreement (God, Christendom, the allies, the allies' retainers);
b) The duration of time for which the agreement would be binding (from the day of its swearing onward);
c) The restraining circumstances or caveats (insofar as God gave the knowledge and the power); and
d) The oath proper (mutual help and support, the avoidance of conduct prejudicial to the alliance).

The retainers' oath is similarly brief and pragmatic, as befitted the circumstances. Without repetition of content, it alludes to the oath already sworn by the brothers, then delineates the circumstances in which each retainer would be obliged to preserve the intent of the agreement (in the case of his leader's breach of faith, each retainer must attempt to deter his leader, but if unsuccessful, must refuse to cooperate with the breach of faith).

Formularism is linked inextricably to functionalism. It was the chancery's responsibility to produce clear, concise documents that would define, prescribe, and delimit while avoiding potentially confusing phraseology. Required also was the ability to accumulate the greatest possible number of formulae in sequence without reaching syntactic saturation.

One feature of the oaths is *not* routine. In his meticulous reconstruction of the chancery process, Alfred Ewert writes, "[O]ne cannot but be struck by the fact that the French version reads awkwardly, presents a number of obscurities and stylistic blemishes, and, in a word, does not read as if it were all of a piece."[12] The German version, on the other hand, appears to have been a faultless conversion, phrase by phrase, of the appropriate formulae. Several of the differences noted by Ewert[13] between the French and German oaths favour Charles, accidentally or not.

There is some logic to the discrepancies. The "awkward repetition" in the French oath forcefully hammers out Louis's commitment to him, *viz.*, he will replace Charles's godfather Lothar as his protector. Louis's new role, which extends beyond *auxilium* (help) to every aspect of the tutelage that Lothar had once promised, is thus spelled out with hyper-explicitness in "si salvarai eo cist meon fradre Karlo et in adjudha et in cadhuna cosa, si cum om per dreit son fradra salvar dift" (I shall succour this my brother Charles both in aid and in everything, as a brother rightly should succour his brother). The oath formalizes the substitution of Louis for Lothar, but there is no actual need for Charles to swear similarly; the reading "non lostanit" may be disputed, but the change of verb is not surprising if Louis's responsibility is to conserve the oath, while Charles's responsibility is perceived differently. In sum, the linguistic differences that Ewert interprets as flaws *could* have arisen merely from an excess of zeal in the French chancery to emphasize Louis's responsibilities to his younger brother.

A number of questions remain unanswered. Was there total incomprehension and incomprehensibility between the German and French armies? Charles was presumably competent in three languages, but what precisely were the linguistic capabilities of the two leaders and their retainers? How to explain the oaths' conservatively Latinate script, which shows no sign of linguistic changes that had almost certainly taken place by 842? And when, definitively, was Romance no longer Latin? That question was posed by Henry F. Muller[14] and by Ferdinand Lot.[15] A response was formulated by Michael Richter.[16] More recently, Roger Wright has reformulated the question because, in his view, the separation of Latin and Romance, precipitated by the Carolingian revival of proper Latin orthography, did not happen much before AD 800. Louis the German may have been more familiar with Latinate pronunciation than with French pronunciation, and the Romance oaths would therefore have been a semi-phonetic reading for a Latin-literate monarch.[17]

A difficulty is inherent in the hypothesis, as Wright himself points out. If the Romance oaths were produced for the benefit of a Germanic speaker who had learned to read Latin but was not fluent in French, that still does not explain why a French phonetic version was provided for the French-speaking army. As Wright says,

> It is not clear why this second Romance oath was written this way; not many of Charles' *populus* could have been likely to be able to read at all, let alone from a baffling orthography that they had not met before. The answer may simply be that once Nithard, or whoever it was, had worked out the first oath for Louis to read, they felt they were sufficiently pleased with what they had achieved to carry on in the same vein for the other

Romance oath, even if strictly it was going to be of less use as Charles'
populus knew French anyway. (p. 125)

This tentative explanation is not fully convincing. Another explanation,
equally tentative, could be proposed, *viz.*, that a non-French-speaking
person, perhaps Louis, had to lead the French army through its declaration of loyalty. If so, phonetic helps would be useful. Nothing would
be more destructive of ceremonial solemnity than to require a French
army to ape alien sounds.

The last phase in the life of the oaths was to ready them for preserva-
tion in the *Histories*, a unique outcome for vernacular documents in the
ninth century. One may reasonably hypothesize that Nithard checked
carefully the words of both vernacular texts before enshrining them in
his work. For this he would access drafts and/or documents from the
chancery – it is inconceivable that he would have made on-the-spot
transcriptions of the actual pledging! It is *not* inconceivable, however,
that he would have reworked or at least repolished the texts somewhat,
which would explain the anomalies in the French text.

Moving from the specifics of the oaths themselves to their function
within the literary context of the *Histories*, it is important to remember
Nithard's own observations. The oaths appear in a part of the *Histories*
that, he says, have now become irksome to him, but he presents them
as inevitable, the logical outcome of all previous events:

Ergo [my emphasis] xvi kal. marcii Lodhuvicus et Karolus in civitate
quę olim Argentaria vocabatur, nunc autem Strazburg vulgo dicitur,
convenerunt et sacramenta quę subter notata sunt, Lodhuvicus romana,
Karolus vero teudisca lingua, juraverunt. (pp. 100–2)

(*Therefore* on 14 February 842 Louis and Charles in the city that was once
called Argentaria but is now commonly known as Strasbourg met and
swore the oaths that are recorded below, Louis in the French and Charles
in the German tongue.)

That initial adverb *ergo* boldly puts the case that Louis the German
and Charles the Bald had no other choice than to formalize an alliance at
Strasbourg. This was the message that Nithard had been commissioned
to present and with which he appears to have concurred, at the beginning anyway. It was a difficult case to present to posterity because it

destroyed the notion of a unified imperium, which, it should be noted, Nithard had initially presented as the ideal model. The presentation had necessitated several strategies: a tedious emphasis upon pledging as the leitmotiv of the first two books; careful characterization of the members of the royal family; and insistence upon the abstractions/ truths that would be invoked at Strasbourg. But by 14 February 842, Nithard is disillusioned, believing that the last useful contribution he made was at the Battle of Fontenoy. He no longer dedicates his prologue to Charles but instead to the readership. The swearing of the oaths *may* have been a logical inevitability. Perhaps they will even serve as a reminder to those who swore them, and certainly they complete the task begun for a now ungrateful monarch. Equally certainly, they are not a glorious climax heralding better times. The negative symbolism of the occasion is unmistakable: in the Latin speech that preceded them, Louis and Charles spoke as one in the official language of the old empire. With the swearing of two separate sets of vernacular oaths in non-Latin tongues, Charlemagne's imperial majesty is over, and the era of Babel has begun.

It is important therefore not to view the oaths through the rose-coloured spectacles of anachronism, looking for the glorious beginnings of France and Germany or the first stirrings of popular language. Occurring in a context of constant pledging, the Strasbourg Oaths were unique only because Nithard made them so. They were inelegant and difficult to read, using languages that were inappropriate in a Latin history; the practical usefulness of the French oath to Charles's *populus* remains unclear, and they started no trend for barbaric quotation among later Latin chroniclers. Nithard's own view of them at this disillusioned time of his life was visibly different from ours. His ideal imperial model was, after all, Karolus Magnus, who according to Nithard earned that designation by imposing unity upon Franks and barbarians alike. Charlemagne spoke Latin as fluently as his own language, a form of Old High German. Indeed, as the written lingua franca, Latin was a crucial administrative tool in Charlemagne's imperium, and Nithard knew as well as anyone the importance that Charlemagne attributed to it, not only for administration but for the promotion of scholarship, and for the correct understanding and pronunciation of texts.[18] On a more personal note, when Nithard's father Angilbert, whom Charlemagne called his dearly beloved abbot – "dilectum abbatum suum"[19] – became abbot of St Riquier, he received from Charlemagne a gospel book (*The Abbéville Gospels*) for the abbey from one of Charlemagne's ateliers.

Nithard, formed and educated in this Latin context and destined soon to retire to St Riquier himself, may well have regarded the now-iconic Strasbourg Oaths as retrogressive rather than progressive, graphic symbols of an empire's decline and vivid representations of all that was wrong with the political world.

This interpretation is supported by the remaining sections of the *Histories*. After Strasbourg, Nithard's fears for the empire multiply incrementally. He has already seen and deplored the irresponsibility of Louis and Charles after Fontenoy, when each returned to his own pursuit of happiness without regard for the public good. The two younger brothers are far from ideal rulers, as Nithard bluntly states when he castigates their neglect of the public interest. In the euphoria of victory, they go their separate ways and pursue their own good pleasure: "Re autem publica inconsultius quam oporteret omissa, quo quemque voluntas rapuit perfacile omissus abscessit" (With unseemly lack of commitment to affairs of state but with very willing commitment to whatever his fancy dictated, each departed, p. 84). Their Fontenoy victory may have been judged by all at the time to be God's vengeance against Lothar, the proof that Louis and Charles were better than their older brother, but this does not dispel Nithard's present concerns.

After Strasbourg, he decribes only one brief oasis of "jolly things worth noting" ("jocunda ac merito notanda," p. 110) during the military games organized by Louis and Charles at Worms for their various constituencies. Saxons, Gascons, Austrasians, and Bretons compete against one other, pursuing one another, then reversing roles and becoming the pursued. Nithard praises the impressive spectacle, the number and diversity of the peoples represented, the fraternal harmony between Louis and Charles, and the restraint with which proceedings are conducted.

This vignette of brotherly love excepted, the reality is less jolly. Negotiations over the repartition of the empire drag on interminably. Louis faces sedition from the Saxons, who, as Nithard sadly reminds his readers, had previously been converted to the true religion by Charlemagne, "justly called *imperator* by all nations" (p. 120). On 5 November 842, the date agreed on for "peace," Nithard inserts an irrelevant eulogy of his father Angilbert, translated on that date to Centulum, the abbey he had built "to the honor of God and St Riquier." It is a significant indicator of Nithard's frame of mind post-Fontenoy.

A non-player in the endless squabbles of Nithard's land-hungry cousins, Angilbert is for Nithard as much an embodiment of perfection as his grandfather Charlemagne, whom he again invokes when he notes that Angilbert and his prominent family were held in deservedly high esteem by the Great Emperor: "apud Magnum Karolum merito magni habebantur" (p. 138). Angilbert built an architectural chef-d'oeuvre, Centulum, to the glory of God and St Riquier; he ruled his family to perfection ("mirifice"); lived in complete felicity ("omni felicitate"); and died in peace ("in pace quievit"). Twenty-nine years[20] later (i.e., October 842) when his body was translated to St Riquier, it was intact, although it had not been embalmed – a sure sign of sanctity. As Charlemagne began the *Histories* as its inspirational father figure and the ikon against whom the present generation is contrasted, the felicitous Angilbert looms unexpectedly over the final pages, dwarfing Nithard's infelicitous, squabbling cousins. Within months, Nithard will follow his revered father to St Riquier.

Nithard's eulogy of Angilbert and his mention of Charlemagne, greatest of all his relatives, brings the narrative full circle. Intoning with the scriptural voice of a prophet – "inquam" (I say unto you) – Nithard warns that rape, plunder, and evils of all sorts are besetting the world. A lunar eclipse, the subsequent snows, and the disastrous climate changes are visible signs of God's wrath. They eliminate all hope that any good can come in the future. The *Histories* end with an apocalyptic quotation from *Sapientia* 5, 21: "Et pugnabit orbis terrarum contra insensatos" (And the earth will war against the foolish). *Ubi est Carolus? Where is Charles?*

Thus, the narrative impetus that carried Nithard towards Strasbourg does not climax triumphally at the end of *the Histories*. Nithard has demonstrated that the Strasbourg Oaths were born out of necessity: *ergo juraverunt*. He has thereby fulfilled his commitment to Charles, but the manner of its fulfilment is ambiguous. For Nithard, the oaths signified no real triumph, and modern anachronistic judgments of them as monuments affirming the emancipation of the French language are inappropriate.

Nithard, writing in his own persona, chose to use Latin, not the vernacular, on the last page of the *Histories* when he prophesied nothing but further dissension and nothing but doom for the dissenters, borrowing the baleful voice of the Old Testament prophets. If his two vernacular quotations were seen by Charles and Louis as a pact to unify kingdoms for the common good, for Nithard they were a graphic representation of the fragmentation of an empire that had been laboriously welded together by an earlier Charles who was *deservedly* called emperor: "merito, magnus imperator ab universis nationibus vocatus" (he was deservedly called great emperor by all nations). Nithard's real voice is audible in his final quotation when, borrowing the Scriptural authority of *The Book of Wisdom*, he mourns the two good men in his family while forecasting never-ending dissension and God's vengeance upon the others: "Et pugnabit orbis terrarum contra insensatos" (And the earth will war against the foolish).

Chapter Two

Whose Words Are They?

Gesta Francorum et aliorum Hierosolimitanorum

The *Gesta Francorum et aliorum Hierosolimitanorum* (*The Deeds of the Franks and Other Crusaders to Jerusalem*) is an eyewitness account of the First Crusade. It appeared anonymously soon after the Battle of Ascalon (12 August 1099), the last major episode of both the Crusade and of the *Gesta*. Biographical facts about the author – and they are scanty – must be gleaned from the narrative itself. For our Anonymous, France was "across the mountains." He came from Italy, a descendant, probably, of a Norman family that had migrated there in the eleventh century. He was a vassal of Bohemond,[1] and saw himself as distinct both from the foot soldiers and from the clergy. Riding with Bohemond's knights, he recorded his experiences faithfully, although not without bias.[2] He was probably a *miles literatus* (educated soldier), but he writes in a manner that would be appreciated as much by fellow *milites* as by *literati*. With the Norman-Italians he crossed over to the Balkan Peninsula, having taken the cross with them in 1096 at Amalfi. He was with Tancred[3] for a time outside Constantinople, then crossed the Bosphorus, took part in the siege of Nicaea, the battle of Dorylaeum, and the two sieges of Antioch. After the capture of Marra, he apparently joined the Provençal army under Raymond of St Gilles, Count of Toulouse,[4] and travelled to Jerusalem, where he fought in the successful attack on that city. All this is recorded sequentially in a narrative that is invaluable for its eyewitness reporting of the First Crusade's major events. It runs the gamut of the Crusading experience: enthusiasm, fear, despair, cool courage, mocking parody of the enemy, humour, and exhilaration. Without loss of control and without sentimentality, our anonymous Crusader shows gratitude for God's help to the army and faith in the rightness of the cause, which for him reached fulfilment at "journey's end."[5]

Literary quotation is rare in this text. There are no suggested comparisons, for example, between Bohemond and Rome's hero Aeneas, and nothing could be further from Anonymous's mind than to validate the First Crusade through classical authority. There *are* Biblical references, reflecting the sort of scriptural knowledge possessed by a committed soldier – which Anonymous patently was.

Its style is simple and direct throughout. It is an easy read, and has no pretensions beyond the narration of experiences of a participant in the First Crusade. Rosalind Hill suggests, interestingly, in the introduction to her 1962 edition and translation that the reactions of soldiers fighting against overwhelming odds in countries near the Mediterranean surely had not varied much between the battle of Marathon and that of al-Alamein, because she finds the *Gesta* comparable in style to an early-twentieth-century letter from the front: "My brother, who had no historical training and had never read the *Gesta*, came extremely close to the style of the book in the letters which he wrote from North Africa in 1942–3."[6] And if Anonymous's narrative reflects nothing of the "boneyard" pessimism that was engendered by the battlefields of the Somme[7] – *his* was a self-imposed pilgrimage and ultimately rewarding – he too conveys by the simplest lexical means the deprivations of a campaign that promised and delivered sickness, hunger, thirst, and all manner of suffering to its participants.

Lexical choices in the *Gesta* show Norman-Italian Romance influence.[8] The syntax is distinctly Romance – Anonymous employs multifunctional "quod" clauses, present participles, gerunds, and infinitives in Romance rather than classical fashion. Typically, he prefers a long series of finite verbs joined by simple connectives over elaborately contrived periodic sentences, and often writes in a style so close to that of popular genres in the vernacular that his narrative has even been described as being in some sense a *chanson de geste*.[9] The author wrote as he thought and if, as is possible, he dictated his words to a scribe, the *Gesta* is in a sense one long quotation.

The circumstances of the *Gesta*'s composition can only be surmised, however, and the degree of Anonymous's literacy cannot be determined with any precision. He may have trained initially as a cleric before taking up a military career. There is only one authorial comment that is remotely relevant. Speaking of the events leading to the capture of Antioch, Anonymous says, "Omnia que egimus antequam urbs esset capta nequeo enarrare, quia nemo est in his partibus, sive clericus sive laicus, qui omnino possit scribere vel narrare sicut res gesta est: tamen aliquantulum dicam" (I am unable to narrate everything we did before the city was captured, because there is no one in these parts, whether cleric or layman, who could record or narrate what happened: nevertheless I shall tell my little bit, p. 100).

From that comment we deduce that when Anonymous "spoke" from "these parts," Antioch had been captured and the Crusade was still in progress. Beyond that nothing is clear, including the implications of the tantalizing phrases "sive clericus sive laicus" (whether cleric or layman), "scribere vel narrare" (write or narrate), and "dicam" (I shall tell), which reveal little about the circumstances of the *Gesta*'s composition. His "Omnia ... nequeo enarrare" (I am unable to narrate everything) is not an admission of failure, however, and his description of the *Gesta* as "aliquantulum" (a little bit), although it employs a diminutive, is not apologetic. It is, rather, his personal variant of two literary conventions, the "modesty topos," which, like most examples of its kind, is not modest at all, and the "inexpressibility topos,"[10] which is similarly self-confident. (It is worth noting that all three of the Crusading chroniclers in this book employ the inexpressibility topos, one of the traditions they share from their common heritage.)[11]

It would be a mistake to take his self-deprecation literally. Despite the inability of an active combatant to register the overall progress of a campaign *in medias res*, Anonymous has remarkable control of the salient facts, and his "aliquantulum" is uniquely authoritative. Furthermore, none of his clerical successors, with all their claims to literary sophistication, matches the authority and the readability of Anonymous's "rustic little book" (as one of its rewriters, Baudri of Bourgeuil, called it).[12] Its authority stems from its author's eyewitness experience of the gruelling hardships it describes; its readability from the fact that he varies the speed of the narrative by interspersing direct speech passages. Inherited rhetorical assumptions about *oratio recta* interact with vernacular techniques of direct reportage as practised in *contes* and *chansons de geste*. One of the most obvious features is, in fact, the frequency of direct speech in the *Gesta*. Unlike Nithard's *Histories*, which employed it only rarely, Anonymous's text weaves in and out of it as readily as if its words were the author's own thoughts – as indeed they are. There are some 97 occurrences of direct speech in the *Gesta Francorum*, a few containing further direct speech within them.[13]

Only one piece of direct speech represents actual words spoken: the Crusaders' battle cry. It is first quoted when Bohemond and Roger of Apulia are laying siege to Amalfi. Bohemond is told of "a countless army of Franks going to Jerusalem"; he inquires about the unknown army, and learns that they are Franks armed for war. They wear Christ's cross on one shoulder or on both, and they cry out with one voice: "Deus le volt! Deus le volt! Deus le volt!" (God wills it! God wills it! God wills it!, p. 18). Anonymous chooses to present the phrase here as a triple utterance shouted in one voice, the stereophonic effect of which reinforces the divine symbolism of "three in one and one in three." Such is its power that Bohemond, moved by the Holy Spirit ("sancto commotus Spiritu"), responds immediately. He orders that the valuable cloak he is wearing be made into crosses, and almost all the soldiers who are there, among them Anonymous, join him, leaving Roger of Apulia to grieve over the loss of his army (p. 20).

The war cry is featured again on the memorable occasion when a handful of Crusaders who are valiantly manning towers in Antioch glimpse the welcome sight of Bohemond's men arriving. The beleaguered band utter the rousing battle cry "jocunda voce" (with joyful voice) and, says Anonymous, who has just arrived with the reinforcements, "we too were crying the same words" (p. 106) as the ascent begins: "Tunc ceperunt illico mirabiliter ascendere" (Then they began the miraculous ascent there, ibid.). The Crusaders manage to scale the towers of Antioch on 3 June 1098, tangible proof for Anonymous that it is God who wills this victory. "Deus le volt," potent in the Crusaders' ascent, remains potent throughout the *Gesta*. This forceful battle cry has a distinctly popular ring, vividly echoing the vernacular because of the demonstrative quality of "le" – "God wills *this/This* is God's will."[14] Anonymous never forgets that the First Crusade is an enterprise that brings together high and low, even speaking their language.

"Deus le volt" aside, no instances of direct speech in the *Gesta* should be understood as *ipsissima verba*, even the words attributed to Pope Urban II at the beginning of the *Gesta*, where Anonymous provides a simple explanation of the origins of the First Crusade. When, he says, the time had come for the fulfilment of Christ's call to the faithful to take up His cross and follow Him, "*Si quis vult post me venire, abneget semetipsum et tollat crucem suam et sequatur me*" (If any man will come after me, let him deny himself, and take up his cross, and follow me, p. 2),[15] there was a powerful movement ("motio valida") throughout the Frankish lands. The pope then preached "ultra montanas partes" (across the mountains)[16] to an assembled group of archbishops, bishops, abbots, and priests. The first sentence of this papal address is presented in indirect speech, the pope urging that anyone who wished to save his soul should not hesitate in all humility to follow the "viam Domini" (the way of the Lord) and, if money was lacking, God's mercy would provide.

The rest of the papal address is presented directly by Anonymous, although he was not present to hear it. It comprises a miscellany of scriptural quotations that would have been familiar to any Crusader – Acts 9:16, II Timothy 1:8, Luke 21:15, Matthew 15:12, and Colossians 3:24. The papal sermon as presented in the *Gesta* derives in fact from Anonymous's own experience of Crusading truths, and he makes no secret of this. Acknowledging that he is providing only the gist of the pope's sermons throughout France, he prefaces his simple report with respectful homage to the pope's preaching through the give-away adverb "subtiliter": "[Apostolicus ... Urbanus] cepit [que] subtiliter sermocinari et predicare, dicens ..." ([Pope ... Urban] began to deliver subtly theological sermons, saying ..., p. 2).

The Crusading precepts upon which the pope is purported to have preached so "subtly" are the necessity for following the way of the Lord in humility, enduring hardship, poverty, nakedness, persecution, deprivation, sickness, hunger, thirst, and all manner of suffering in the name of Christ:

> Fratres, vos oportet multa pati pro nomine Christi, videlicet miserias, paupertates, nuditates, persecutiones, egestates, infirmitates, fames, sites et alia hujusmodi, sicuti Dominus ait suis discipulis: *Oportet vos pati multa pro nomine meo* et: *Nolite erubescere loqui ante facies hominum; ego vero dabo vobis os et eloquium* ac deinceps: *Persequetur vos larga retributio.* (p. 4)

> (Brethren, it behooves you in Christ's name to suffer many things, namely misery, poverty, nakedness, persecutions, indigence, infirmities, hunger, thirst, and other such things, as the Lord said to his disciples: *You must suffer much for my name's sake* and: *Do not be ashamed to speak before the faces of men; for I will give you a mouth and eloquence* and further: *Great reward will follow you.*)

This unsubtle version of the papal sermon has its own authenticity, conveying Anonymous's understanding of the responsibilities of the Crusaders, *viz.*, innumerable hardships coupled with a great reward ("larga retributio"). Suffering and recompense are an integral part of the narrative, and Anonymous's version of the papal address is thus a serviceable introduction to, and validation of, the *Gesta* as well as the First Crusade.

Significantly, the papal sermon as "quoted" by Anonymous is no more or less authoritative than the same papal sermon as later "quoted" by chroniclers with more literary pretensions. Robert the Monk, for example, was commissioned by his abbot to rewrite the *Gesta* by virtue of the fact that he was an eyewitness at the Council of Clermont (although not of the First Crusade itself), and also because the abbot opined that the *Gesta* was uncouth, with neither a proper beginning nor sophistication of style: "Praecepit igitur mihi ut, qui Clari Montis concilio interfui, acephalae materiei caput praeponerem et lecturis eam accuratiori stili componerem"[17] (He instructed me therefore, because I was present at the Council of Clermont, to supply the acephalous stuff with a head [i.e., preface] and to compose it in a more studied style for future readers' sake).

Robert's papal address is substantially longer than that in the *Gesta*, but neither his version nor those of the other three eyewitness clerics is any more trustworthy. Each is different; each chronicler introduces themes that will be appropriate for his own chronicle, and three of the four indicate, like Anonymous, that their reporting of the sermon is a reconstruction. Robert reports that the pope delivered "these words and many others in similar vein";[18] Baudri de Bourgeuil says "these things or others of the same sort were said";[19] and Guibert de Nogent says the pope used "even if not these words, these intentions."[20] Early in the last century, D.C. Munro attempted a reconstruction of the content of Urban II's speech by comparing the versions of Robert the Monk, Baudri of Bourgeuil, Fulcher of Chartres, Guibert of Nogent, and William of Malmesbury. In his tentative summary, he prints the subjects about which there seem to be no doubt without inclosures, and those that the pope probably used in parentheses; those that he may have used are in brackets:

[Praise of the valor of the Franks]; necessity of aiding the brethren in the East; appeals for aid from the East; victorious advance of the Turks; [reference to Spain]; sufferings of the Christians in the East; (sufferings of the pilgrims); desecration of the churches and holy places; [expressions of contempt concerning the Turks]; special sanctity of Jerusalem; this is God's work; (rich and poor to go); grant of plenary indulgence; fight righteous wars instead of iniquitous combats; (evil conditions at home); promise of eternal and temporal rewards; let nothing hinder you; God will be your leader.[21]

This attempted reconstruction was based upon Munro's (anachronistic) assumptions about direct speech in the early Crusading historians, however. To arrive at the presumed intent and content of Pope Urban II's speech, a more reliable approach has been to work with the material from Urban's own hand: the canons from the Council of Clermont reconstructed by Robert Somerville and his own letter referencing the journey.[22] A further promising line of development is the study of evidence from the charters issued by Crusaders, mostly to raise money for their journeys, in the period immediately or very soon after the council.[23] For, as Jonathan Riley-Smith nicely summarizes it, "we cannot … put much trust in the four eyewitness accounts of his sermon to the council of Clermont which were written by memory after 1099."[24] At least Anonymous modestly indicates the summary nature of his version by acknowledging that, unlike Anonymous himself, the pope preached it subtly.

The fictive role of direct speech in the *Gesta* is illustrated even more dramatically in the cries of the poor Crusaders who died of starvation during the siege of Nicaea (June 1097), put on robes of martyrdom, and called in unison from heaven: "Vindica, Domine, sanguinem nostrum, qui pro te effusus est, qui es benedictus et laudabilis in secula seculorum. Amen" (Avenge, Oh Lord, the blood we have shed for Thee, blessed and worthy of praise, world without end. Amen, p. 42).

It is patently obvious that Anonymous did not figure personally in the heavenly throng any more than he sat with the bishops and archbishops at Clermont. The pleas of dead Crusaders in heaven do not represent historical fact. Nevertheless, the semi-scriptural quotation[25] has its own veracity, transcending its source to provide a glimpse of the Crusading army's view that they were a part of salvation history. In this, of course, they were no different from their enemies.[26] Anonymous parodies *that* delusion in a gleeful fantasy aping the pagan enemy's thoughts and words (see this volume, pp. 32–4).

Direct speech in the *Gesta* ranges far beyond scriptural allusion.[27] The length of its manifestations also varies widely, from short (the three words "Deus le volt") to long (the lively dialogue between Kerbogha[28] and his mother [see this volume, pp. 34–5]). Some direct speech passages move the narrative forward when Anonymous has only a modicum of information. He was not privy to the negotiations of his leaders, for example, but produces a single utterance from them that cuts through a set of unknown details to give the outcome of a Crusading council of war before Antioch in December 1097. The leaders announce,

"Faciamus castrum in vertice montis Maregart, quo securi atque tuti possimus esse a Turcorum formidine" (Let us make a camp at the top of Mount Maregart so that we can be safe and free from fear of the Turks, p. 70). The building of the proposed camp is then conveyed by an ablative absolute of five words, "Facto itaque castro atque munito" (The camp having been built and fortified). No sooner have the leaders uttered a suggestion than it is done! Anonymous then moves quickly to soldierly matters of more interest to him, continuing the main narrative inexorably.

The use of direct speech is discretionary. *Indirect* reporting conveys both the Emperor Alexius's agreement with Godfrey of Bouillon[29] (p. 18) and Alexius's instructions to provide the Crusaders with safe conduct (p. 24). It is not the material that determines the choice but the narrator's interest in, or attitude to, that material. The mini-drama enacting the quarrel between Tancred and Baldwin[30] over Tarsus dramatizes the psychological conflict between two warlords, and crystallizes the points of view of the two rivals. The protagonists are the "noble" Baldwin, who desires cooperation, and the "heroic" Tancred, who is motivated by pride but also (eventually) reasonableness. The backdrop is Tarsus, whose inhabitants shout an invitation to the "invincible" Franks to come into their city. Brief pointers (climate indicators, if one may so label them) ensure an appropriate appreciation of the scene (I have italicized them in the following passage):

[V]enit Balduinus comes cum suo exercitu postulans Tancredum quatinus eum *amicissime* in societatem civitatis dignaretur suscipere; cui ait Tancredus: "Te omnimodo in hac societate denego." Nocte itaque superveniente, omnes Turci *tremefacti* fugam una arripuerunt. Exierunt denique habitatores civitatis sub illa noctis obscuritate, *clamantes excelsa voce*: "Currite, *invictissimi* Franci, currite, quia Turci *expergefacti* vestro timore omnes pariter recedunt." Orta autem die, venerunt majores civitatis et reddiderunt *sponte* civitatem, dicentes illis qui super hoc litigabant adinvicem: "Sinite modo, seniores, sinite, quia volumus et petimus dominari et regnare super nos illum qui heri *tam viriliter* pugnavit cum Turcis." Balduinus itaque, *mirificus* comes, altercabatur et litigabat cum Tancredo, dicens: "Intremus simul et spoliemus civitatem et qui plus potuerit habere, habeat, et qui poterit capere, capiat." Cui *fortissimus* Tancredus dixit: "Absit hoc a me. Ego namque christianos nolo exspoliare; homines hujus civitatis elegerunt me dominum super se meque habere desiderant." Tandem nequivit *vir fortis* Tancredus diu luctari cum Balduino comite quia illi magnus erat exercitus; tamen volens nolensque dimisit eam et *viriliter* recessit cum suo exercitu. (p. 58)

(Then Count Baldwin came with his army requesting that Tancred deign to share the city *amicably*; Tancred said to him: "I absolutely refuse this association with you." Night intervened and all the Turks *fled in terror*. Then the inhabitants of Tarsus emerged under cover of darkness, *shouting at the top of their voices*: "Come in, *unconquered* Franks, come in. The *terrified* Turks are afraid of you and are all retreating." When dawn came, the important men of Tarsus came and *spontaneously* handed over the city, saying to those who were squabbling over it: "Stop, gentlemen stop. We want as our lord and ruler the man who fought so *heroically* yesterday against the Turks." *The magnificent* Count Baldwin continued to argue and dispute with Tancred, saying: "Let's go in together and pillage the city; whoever can take the most, let him take it, and whoever can capture, let him capture." The *superbly brave* Tancred said: "Far be it from me. I do not wish to plunder Christians. The men of this city have chosen me and want to have me as their lord." Finally, however, *the brave* Tancred gave up the struggle with Count Baldwin who had a large army; willy-nilly, he left the city and *courageously* withdrew with his army.)

These brief exchanges do not represent a word-for-word report, but are an economical means to record a serious dispute with racy immediacy. Anonymous is a born storyteller.

Psychological profiling of the Norman leader Bohemond is achieved in similar fashion. A mini-drama outside Antioch in February 1098 (pp. 82–4) conveys the trepidation of the Crusaders at the magnitude of the Turkish threat, the superb leadership of Bohemond as he reassures his men, and the respect Bohemond inspires in them, which approaches adulation: "Seniores et prudentissimi milites, quid facturi erimus? ... Faciamus ex nobis duas partes ..." (My lords, my very skilled soldiers, what are we to do? ... Let's divide into two sections ...). The scouts then warn of an impending Turkish attack: "Ecce, ecce veniunt!" (Look, look, they're coming!), which brings an immediate order from the wise ("sapiens") Bohemond: "Seniores et invictissimi milites, ordinate adinvicem bellum" (My lords, my always victororious soldiers, draw up your battle lines). The army then apostrophizes him in unison: "Tu sapiens et prudens, tu magnus et magnificus, tu fortis et victor, tu bellorum arbiter et certaminum judex, hoc totum fac, hoc totum super te sit, omne bonum quod tibi videtur, nobis et tibi operare fac" (Oh, shrewd and wise, great and magnificent, strong and victorious, planner and judge of battles, do all this, take charge of it all, do whatever seems good to you, and command this operation for your sake and ours).

Of all the direct exchanges reported above, only the scouts' shout of warning might conceivably be close to actual words uttered. There is no way that Bohemond could take time to explain the Crusaders are outnumbered; ask them – then tell them – in measured tones ("caute") what to do; and hear them out as they apostrophize him in unison, while all of this time, "numberless" Turks are attacking. "Wise" Bohemond's direct address and his men's responding paean of praise convey more important realities, *viz.*, that Bohemond had leadership qualities and that those who fought with him, not least Anonymous, fully supported him.

Direct speech highlights the realities of treachery as effectively as the realities of hero worship. Tatikios, official representative and envoy of Alexius, is as mistrusted by the Crusaders as is the iniquitous emperor ("imperator iniquus"). According to Anonymous, Tatikios is so cowardly that he abandons the Crusaders during their time of dire hardship outside Antioch (February 1098). Before leaving them, he promises to arrange delivery of all the supplies so desperately needed by the suffering army. The "mendacious" Tatikios's speech to the Crusaders, prefaced with its warning indicators "*inimicus* Tatikios, *fingens omnia falsa*" (our enemy Tatikios, fabricating a bunch of lies) documents the promises that were so generously laced with earnest assurances of good faith – a list of the commitments that he failed to honour:

> Interea inimicus Tetigus ..., fingens omnia falsa, dixit; "Seniores et viri prudentissimi, videte quia nos sumus hic in maxima necessitate et ex nulla parte nobis adjutorium succedit; ecce modo sinite me in Romanie patriam reverti et ego absque ulla dubitatione faciam huc multas naves venire per mare, onustas frumento, vino, hordeo, carne, farina et caseis omnibusque bonis que sunt nobis necessaria; faciam et equos conduci ad vendendum et mercatum per terram in fidelitate imperatoris huc advenire. Ecce hec omnia vobis fideliter jurabo et attendam; adhuc quoque et domestici mei et papilio meus sunt in campo, unde et formiter credite quia quantocius redibo." (pp. 78–80)

> (Meanwhile Tatikios our enemy ..., fabricating a bunch of lies, said, "My lords and most valiant men, you see we are in dire straits and no aid is getting to us from anywhere. So let me return to the country of Romania,

and I shall arrange without delay for many ships to come here by sea, loaded with grain, wine, barley, meat, flour, cheese, and all the goods that we need; I shall have horses brought here to be sold and merchandise transported across the emperor's territory. See all the things that I shall swear faithfully to you and arrange; my household and my tent are still in the camp, so believe resolutely that I shall return.")

Because in the narrative Tatikios's promises issue directly from his own lips, they are more reprehensible in the breach, so many indictments for which Tatikios must personally answer. Anonymous damns him for guaranteeing food and supplies to a needy army, only to abandon his promises later. His perjury was unforgivable and, Anonymous says, Tatikios "in perjurio manet et manebit" (Tatikios remains and will remain in a state of perjury).

(Not surprisingly, Greek versions of Tatikios's departure from Antioch differ from that of the *Gesta*. Anna Comnena claims that Bohemond coveted Antioch for himself, and, reluctant to hand it over to Tatikios as promised, falsely reported – Anna presents the report in direct speech – that there was a plot against Tatikios's life. Tatikios then fled in terror and Bohemond, already characterized in *The Alexiad* as a natural liar, spelled out to the counts of the Crusading army – in direct speech – his plan to conquer Antioch.[31] Anonymous was not the only historian to use direct speech to propagandist effect; the device was equally persuasive whether it demonstrated Greek or Frankish perfidy!)

Curiously, the *Gesta*'s 1924 editor, Louis Bréhier, hypothesizes that the lengthier examples of direct speech were not written by Anonymous. He posits that the *Gesta* had not one but *two* Anonymi, a Crusading Norman knight and a clerical ghostwriter who added what Bréhier calls "hors-d'oeuvres":

[L]'analyse du texte nous révèle la collaboration d'un chevalier, à qui l'on doit le récit des faits dont il a été le témoin oculaire ou sur lesquels il a pu se procurer des renseignements précis, et d'un clerc qui a voulu enrichir ces données à sa manière par des amplifications d'un caractère oratoire, dont les thèmes lui étaient fournis par sa connaissance des Ecritures et de la littérature populaire, aussi abondante en Occident qu'à Byzance, relative aux musulmans. (pp. vii–viii)

(Analysis of the text reveals the collaboration of a knight, who is responsible for the narrative of the events he witnessed or about which he was

able to acquire precise information, and a cleric who wished to enrich
these materials in his own way with rhetorical amplifications, the themes
of which came from his knowledge of Scripture and of the popular literature, as rich in the West as in Byzantium, pertaining to the Muslims.)

Bréhier even challenges Anonymous's authorship of a five-line command from Bohemond to his constable Robert fitzGerard when the
Crusaders are being pushed back in a particularly vigorous attack by
the Turks outside Antioch. Bohemond, groaning, urges his constable to
advance as quickly as possible, and "be the best athlete for Christ," a
favoured Crusading metaphor:

> Vade quam citius potes, ut vir fortis, et esto acer in adjutorium Dei Sanc-
> tique Sepulcri, et revera scias quia hoc bellum non est carnale, sed spiri-
> tuale. Esto igitur fortissimus athleta Christi! Vade in pace; Dominus sit
> tecum ubique! (p. 84)

> (Charge ahead as fast as you can, like the brave man you are. Fight ac-
> tively for God and the Holy Sepulchre, and know for truth that this war is
> not carnal but spiritual. So be the very best athlete for Christ! Go in peace
> and may God be with you wherever you go!)

Bréhier says of this speech that "la véracité est plus que suspecte, [et]
trahit certainement le langage d'un clerc" (its veracity is more than suspect [and] smacks of a *clerc*'s language, p. 85, n. 3).

Bréhier's hypothesis is not based upon any codicological evidence,
but upon a set of presuppositions that can be summarized as follows:
Bréhier believes Anonymous to have been by temperament terse and
factual; some parts of the *Gesta* are not terse and factual; therefore they
are not by Anonymous. This argument is circular, and it imposes sub-
jectively anachronistic expectations upon a medieval work. Unfortunately, it has led to further anachronistic hypotheses. In 1928, August
Krey criticized "the tangled fashion" in which Anonymous reported
the outcome of a leaders' council (at which he was not, of course, present). Krey proposed, again without codicological evidence, that a passage in the *Gesta* containing promises from Alexius to Bohemond was
a late insertion serving to promote Bohemond's recruitment drive for
his 1107 campaign against the Byzantine emperor. Sympathizing with
Anonymous's frustration with the leaders' negotiations, but finding the

praise for Bohemond an incoherent element, Krey hypothesized further that there may have been other passages favourable to Bohemond inserted later for propaganda purposes: "[T]he process of adapting the work for the recruiting campaign may have led to other changes in the original text. In this it supports Bréhier's thesis of multiple or at least dual authorship for the work as we have it."[32]

Behind Bréhier's and Krey's hypotheses about authorship (two Anonymi according to Bréhier, three and possibly more according to Krey) are anachronistic expectations. Krey's hypothesis, inspired by early-twentieth-century uses of the written word for war propaganda, is discussed and dismissed in a recent article by Nicholas Paul.[33] Bréhier's original hypothesis, upon which Krey based *his* hypothesis, has also been challenged by H.J. Witzel in his 1952 dissertation,[34] and in a follow-up article[35] where he calls for a detailed study of the composition and style of the *Gesta*:

> Jusqu'ici le problème de l'auteur des *Gesta Francorum* n'a été étudié que par des historiens. Comme la solution du problème peut être fournie par la critique stylistique, il serait souhaitable qu'un médiolatiniste compétent se livrât à un examen approfondi, systématique et détaillé de la composition et du style de cette source.
>
> Il n'y a pas que des tournures rédactionnelles qui lui offriraient le matériel de recherche requis. Ce n'est qu'après une étude soigneuse du vocabulaire, de la syntaxe et des figures de rhétorique employés par l'Anonyme qu'on pourra déterminer si celui-ci est l'auteur unique des *Gesta Francorum*. Ce ne sera alors qu'on pourra atteindre à une interprétation vraiment satisfaisante d'une de nos plus importantes sources pour l'histoire de la première croisade. (p. 328)

(Until now the problem of the *Gesta Francorum*'s authorship has been studied only by historians. Since the problem is soluble through stylistic criticism, it would be desirable for a competent medieval Latinist to undertake a detailed in-depth study of the composition and style of this source. The material for this much-needed inquiry goes far beyond formalized idioms. Only after a careful study of the vocabulary, syntax, and figures of speech employed by Anonymous will one be able to determine whether he is the sole author of the *Gesta Francorum*. Only then will a truly satisfactory interpretation be possible of one of our most important historical sources for the First Crusade.)

While it is not possible in the space of this chapter to provide the full stylistic analysis suggested by Witzel, some comment on Bréhier's "non-veracious" passages is relevant because, significantly, all of them involve direct or indirect reporting of speeches. Analysis reveals that there no difference lexically or stylistically between these so-called "hors d'oeuvres" and the rest of the *Gesta*. Sentences feature multi-functional "quod" clauses and are joined by simple connectives. They feature the same proportion of present participles, gerunds, and infinitives. Length is not achieved by any elaborately contrived period. There is no artificial attempt to depart from the word order of Romance. Adjectives and adverbs continue to be used sparingly to convey crucial attributes and to ensure an appropriate assessment of a character/situation. Superlatives are frequent, as is hyperbole. Stylistic devices are simple: alliteration, assonance, and rhyme.[36] Literary allusion is present only through the biblical phrases that were common Crusading parlance, a type of automatic quotation that also accounts for the metaphors he employed. Most crucial of all, perhaps, these passages contain the same type of (mis)information about the enemy that is found in the *chansons de geste* that decry, for example, the "pagan" Saracens' worship of idols and pagan polytheism.[37] The passages Bréhier finds suspect are Soliman II's speech to the Arabs after Dorylaeum; the details of negotiations between the Turkish emirs and Kerbogha to aid Antioch, and Kerbogha's letter to the Caliph; the dialogue between Kerbogha and his mother; and the lament of the Egyptian emir after Ascalon. As their context makes clear, none of these passages pretends to be eyewitness reporting.

In the first, 10,000 Arabs question (in unison?) a terrified Soliman II as he flees the Crusading army after the Turks' defeat at Dorylaeum (1 July 1097): "O infelix et infelicior omnibus gentibus, cur tremefactus fugis?" (Wretched man, more wretched than anyone in the world, why are you fleeing in terror?, p. 52). Soliman answers tearfully ("lacrimabiliter") that countless hordes of invincible Franks have scared the Turks out of their minds, and are now ready to slaughter all in their path. A 13-line description of these numberless Franks uses the same hyperbolic terminology, it should be noted, that was used a few pages before for the numberless Turks, Arabs, and Saracens who confronted the Crusaders before Dorylaeum. Having been invited, in epic fashion, to envisage the scene in which "you or anyone who had been there would think that all the mountains and hills and valleys and all the plains were covered with the host of them" ("si vos aut aliquis illic adesset, putaret quod

omnes montes et colles vallesque et omnia plana loca plena essent illo-
rum multitudine," p. 52), the 10,000 Arabs prudently disperse, leaving
the "invincible" Franks to pursue the "iniquitous" Turks.

Some months later, when Bohemond and his men have established
themselves in Antioch, Sensadolus (Schems-ed-daoula), the son of the
emir who had been placed in charge of that city, pleads tearfully ("lac-
rimando") with Kerbogha, the emir of Mosul (and potentially one of
the Crusaders' most dangerous enemies), for assistance against the
"invincible" Franks. They negotiate to and fro and Kerbogha agrees to
give assistance. Then follows a provocative little *mise en scène* in which
the Turks joke with Kerbogha about the Crusaders' outmoded weapons
and show him a cheap, rusty sword, a blackened old bow, and an old-
fashioned lance absconded (Anonymous takes care to say) from poor
pilgrims ("nuper pauperibus peregrinis"): "Ecce arma que attulerunt
Franci obviam nobis ad pugnam" (Look at the weapons that the Franks
have brought to fight us, p. 116). Kerbogha smiles at this and proclaims
boastfully:

> Hec sunt arma bellica et nitida que attulerunt Christiani super nos in
> Asiam, quibus putant nos et confidunt expellere ultra confinia Corrozane
> et delere omnia nomina nostra ultra Amazonia flumina, qui propulerunt
> omnes parentes nostros a Romania et Antiochia urbe regia, que est hon-
> orabile caput totius Syrie? (p. 116)

> (Are these are the fierce and shining weapons that the Christians have
> brought to conquer us in Asia, the arms with which they confidently be-
> lieve they will drive us out of Khorassan and wipe out our name beyond
> the rivers of the Amazons, those Christians who expelled all our relatives
> from Romania and from the royal city of Antioch, magnificent capital of
> all Syria?)

He then dictates a 26-line letter to "our apostolic caliph," pledging
"by Mahomet and the names of all our gods" the destruction of the
Franks wherever they may have trespassed. The letter uses the protocol
of Latin charts and Latin institutions, but humourously instructs "our
apostolic caliph" and his minions "to be happy, rejoice in jolly unity,
and fill their bellies to satiation." It ends grandiosely, with an oath in
the name of "Mahomet and all our gods" swearing not to appear before
the apostolic caliph until he has conquered for him not only Antioch
but the whole of Syria, Romania, Bulgaria, and *even as far as Apulia* (my

emphasis; Anonymous's compatriots would surely enjoy this local reference!). The letter contains the usual assumptions of its time, some commonly held (that the Muslims were polytheistic), some less current (that the tenth-century wars of Nicephorus Phocas and John Tzimisces were a Frankish enterprise rather than a Byzantine). It has not been produced, obviously, from a *bona fide* document, but from Anonymous's imagination (although Bréhier unexpectedly judges the dialogue between Sensadolus and Kerbogha to be acceptable because it could have been reported to the Crusading army by spies).[38]

After Kerbogha's boastful pledge to demolish all the Franks to a man, his mother engages him in a lengthy dialogue, pleading tearfully with him not to engage with the Franks "in the names of all our gods" (pp. 118–124). Showing an improbably detailed knowledge of Christian belief, and quoting from scripture, she tells him that the sons of Christ have a God who watches over them like a shepherd. She prophesies that if Kerbogha *does* take them on, he cannot fail to incur great damage and shame, lose his faithful soldiers, and forfeit all the splendid booty he has amassed. He will eventually turn tail and flee in fear beyond measure:

> Hoc autem, carissime, in rei veritate scias, quoniam isti Christiani filii Christi vocati sunt et, prophetarum ore, *filii adoptionis et promissionis* et secundum Apostolum *heredes Christi sunt*, quibus Christus hereditates repromissas jam donavit dicendo per prophetas: *A solis ortu usque ad occasum erunt termini vestri et nemo stabit contra vos.* (p. 120)

> (Know this for truth, dearest son, those Christians are called the sons of Christ and, by the word of the prophets, *the sons of adoption and of promise* and, according to the Apostle, *the heirs of Christ.* To them Christ has already given the inheritance he promised when he said through the prophets: *From the rising to the setting of the sun will be your boundaries and nobody will stand against you.*)

These emotional exchanges between Kerbogha, who is moved to the depths of his being ("dolens intimis visceribus"), and his tearful mother, whom he accuses of being crazy and possessed by the furies, contain obviously morale-boosting praise for the Christians. The scene ends with campfire humour: Kerbogha's mother leaves unsuccessful, but her distress at her son's behaviour does not prevent her from filching from the citadel. She returns to Aleppo, "deferens secum cuncta spolia que conducere potuit" (taking with her all the goodies she was able to carry back, p. 124). The episode is an audience-pleaser, deriding the emotionalism and avarice of the enemy while lauding God's fearless army.

Finally, after Ascalon, the *Gesta* features a lament from the Egyptian emir after his defeat by "tantilla gente christianorum" (by such a wretched little band of Christians, p. 216). The emir's exotic outpouring of grief and his uncontrolled weeping at the triumph of a miserable bunch of unarmed mendicants convey the incredulous exhilaration of the Crusading army at their triumph. The emir, distraught at being "dishonored throughout the land of Babylon," vows never to employ mercenaries or pour money into war machines again. There is no way that any Christian participant in the First Crusade could have claimed eyewitness experience of these dramatic episodes, but the passages have their own veracity.

The content and attitudes of these narrative developments visibly owe much to vernacular *chanson de geste* traditions. Bréhier's fanciful hypothesis that they were rhetorical amplifications by a second Anonymous derive from his misguided assumptions about direct speech. Disregarding the literary context of early history-writing, Bréhier clearly wishes to regard Anonymous as a modern historian *avant la lettre*.[39] His editorial comment on Anonymous's unique quotation of an alien vernacular – medieval Greek – betrays his anachronistic expectations regarding medieval history-writing. The quotation occurs just before the scaling of the Antioch towers, and is purportedly spoken by Firouz, Bohemond's Turkish ally, who has just treacherously delivered his Antioch towers over to 60 of Bohemond's men. Firouz at that moment becomes fearful, and utters three Greek words: "Micro Francos echome." The three words are immediately explained: "hoc est: paucos Francos habemus" (that is: we have few Franks, p. 106). The narration then reverts to Latin.

In his 1890 edition of the *Gesta*,[40] Hagenmayer questioned the authenticity of Firouz's Greek comment. Bréhier, byzantinist and historian, did *not* question its veracity: "Il n'y a aucune raison pour mettre en doute, comme le veut Hagenmeyer ... la véracité de la réflexion de Firouz. Le grec était resté en Orient une langue internationale et beaucoup de Turcs le parlaient" (There is no reason to cast doubt, as does Hagenmeyer, on the authenticity of Firouz's comment. Greek had remained an international language in the East and many Turks spoke it, p. 107, n1). Bréhier accepts the Greek phrase on the grounds that because the historical Firouz *could have* uttered a sentence in Greek, Firouz therefore *did*. (He does not address the question of which of his two Anonymi, the first or the hypothetical second, produced the Greek phrase.) Unfortunately, both editors are asking – and answering – the wrong question, *viz.*, whether Firouz the Turk could have known Greek. Their editorial disagreement over "Micro Francos echome" reveals the dangers of anachronistic criteria when assessing textual rightness or wrongness. (Now it would be editorial protocol, anyway, to accept the *lectio difficilior* [the more difficult reading]!). One thing can be guaranteed: we have no way of knowing now whether or not three Greek words were actually uttered by Firouz when he saw a paltry 60 Crusaders manning his towers, but we *can* assess the effect produced in the narrative by this sudden piece of Greek in the middle of Firouz's Latin discourse. A literary choice, it contributes to Anonymous's presentation of the *historia* of which it is an integral part.

In its context, Firouz's unexpected switch to another language ruptures a narration in which everything about Firouz's cooperation had appeared to be proceeding smoothly. "Ordinata sunt denique hec omnia" (Finally all this was in order, p. 104). Bohemond offers the comment – in direct speech – that with God's favour, Antioch will that night be theirs: "Favente Dei gratia, hac nocte tradetur nobis Antiochia" (ibid.). But then Firouz has a panic attack over his tenuous situation. He has alienated himself from the Turks but is not truly part of a Crusading victory. His sudden fear – and Anonymous's contempt for it – is impressionistically conveyed by his unexpected three-word phrase in the language of a people who in the *Gesta*[41] and in the Middle Ages generally are mocked for their effeminacy and unmanliness. "Micro Francos echome" is the caricaturist's thought bubble above Firouz's head. It transmits his fear graphically in the appropriate language for fear. In the next cartoon frame, Firouz reverts to the appropriate language for the occasion, and calls for the star of this Latin show: "Ubi est acerrimus Boamundus? Ubi est ille invictus?" (Where is the splendid Bohemond? Where is that conquering hero?, p. 106). Bohemond's heroic response (urged on, it should be added, by one of the heroic Longobard companion-soldiers) is, of course, predictable. Bohemond and the Crusaders, including Anonymous, scale the towers and massacre all who oppose them, even Firouz's brother. (Firouz's fearful Greek moment was not unjustified, it was merely misdirected!)

It would be a pity on grounds of inauthenticity to follow Bréhier and question the veracity of such spicy "hors d'oeuvres." Short or long, they accurately reflect a soldier's healthy caricature of a foreign enemy, puffed up with self-importance, hysterical with fear, lacrimose at the prospect of – and after experiencing – defeat. These episodes would – and perhaps did – make for excellent campfire entertainment, but Bréhier grants authenticity only to those direct speech passages that seem to him "probable" (i.e., actually spoken). To call into question the reliability of the otherwise trusted Anonymous in this way is to impose limitations upon his individuality as a reporter of Crusading experiences – *and* to misunderstand the function of direct speech.

In sum, the unstudied nature of the *Gesta*'s narrative style does not change, whatever the mode. Anonymous is narrating his own account of events, which he believes to be epic in importance. In his lived epic, the chief participants are "nos" (we) and "nostri" (our side). Their leader Bohemond has their undivided loyalty.[42] The history/story combines the terse succinctness of a soldier who has experienced fear and hardship with a morale-boosting humour that serves to reduce a formidable enemy to size. The epic conventions that Anonymous employs will, he knows, resonate with his contemporaries, and curiously, he makes no mention of writing for posterity. Ironically, posterity has judged his history to be supremely authoritative from the twelfth century onwards.[43] And if his simple approach did not win universal favour in clerical circles, his narrative was nevertheless used, warts and all, by subsequent rehandlers, many of them with greater pretensions who wrote longer, although not intrinsically better, histories of the First Crusade. It is remarkable also that all of those rehandlers, even the two chroniclers who were themselves participants in the Crusade, recognized Bréhier's so-called "hors-d'oeuvres" for what they were: an integral part of the narrative. Thus the ultimate triumph was his, and the "rusticity" of the *Gesta* still wears well, having even in the twenty-first century a ring of veracity. This in spite of, or rather *because of*, its practices of quotation.

Chapter Three

Villehardouin "Who Never, to the Best of His Knowledge, Spoke an Untrue Word"

La Conquête de Constantinople

Geoffroy de Villehardouin's *La Conquête de Constantinople*[1] is the first French prose history extant. Its author was born around 1148. His name is listed among the vassals of the Count of Champagne in 1172 as "Godfridus de Villehardouin ligius et debet Trecis custodiam" (Geoffrey of Villehardouin, liegeman in Troyes) and in 1185–6 as advisor to the countess Marie de Champagne as "Gaufridus marescallus" (Geoffrey the marshal). He continued in his role of marshal as "comitis Henrici marescaldus" (marshal to Count Henry [II]), then as "Campanie marescallus" (marshal of Champagne), then as "marescallus comitis Theobaldi" (marshal to Count Thibaut). He was named as one of the pledges for the young Thibaut III when the latter was recognized as liegeman of Philip Augustus in April 1198. Persuaded by the preaching of Fulk of Neuilly, he took the cross, along with Count Thibaut of Champagne and Count Louis of Blois, and the many others he names at the beginning of his history (paras. 3–10). He was chosen as one of the leaders and chief negotiators of the Fourth Crusade, ordering as well as participating in the action. In April 1202 the "marescallus quondam Campaniae" (the once marshal of Champagne) then ordered his affairs to take on, in 1204, the wider responsibilities of "marshal of Romania."[2] Visibly a familiar of the aristocracy and one of the nobles' most trusted representatives for many years, it was in a context of high nobility that he served faithfully,[3] and it was for this same context that he recorded what he saw.

It was an informed audience, sophisticated although not necessarily Latin-literate, and necessarily involved and interested in the historical details of the most important event in their lifetimes. And because his audience knew his diplomatic and military skills, Villehardouin does not hesitate to remind them that his work has the authority of an author "qui a toz les conseils fu" (who was present at all the councils). He was proud of his eyewitness experience. His personal and passionate commitment to the expedition from its problematic beginnings to its disheartening finish clearly determined the direction of his chronicle, in which, however, he affirms that he never deviated by one word from the truth ("que ainc n'i menti de mot a son escient").

Villehardouin's truthful intent became an issue early in the twentieth century, when Albert Pauphilet[4] contrasted *La Conquête de Constantinople* by Robert de Clari, "ce naïf auteur" (that naïf author), and *La Conquête de Constantinople* by Villehardouin, "[qui] a dit la vérité, mais ... ne l'a pas toute dite" ([who] spoke the truth but not the whole truth). Noting Villehardouin's reticence on certain subjects, he opined that Robert de Clari's chief merit was his absolute sincerity: "On admet que le principal mérite de la relation que nous a laissée Robert de Clari de la IVe Croisade est sa parfaite sincérité" (Admittedly the main value of the report Robert de Clari left us of the Fourth Crusade is its total sincerity). Pauphilet accused Villehardouin of disingenuousness because "avec une rare adresse, il a reconstitué une suite plausible de faits d'où les points délicats étaient éliminés" (with rare skill, he reconstructed a plausible sequence of events from which the sensitive details were eliminated).

Edmond Faral responded to Pauphilet's accusation with an article that defended Villehardouin's reputation without claiming to defend "une manière d'écrire l'histoire qui ne répond plus à nos exigences d'esprit" (a type of history-writing that no longer fits our intellectual demands, p. 581).[5] For Faral, the key issue in his moral defence of Villehardouin's probity was whether the marshal suppressed any information: "Pour en décider, il faut avant tout savoir si, en effet, il a caché quelque chose. On a cherché. On a cru découvrir certains faits dont il est exact qu'il n'a point parlé: vérification faite, ces faits sont imaginaires" (To reach a conclusion, one must first ascertain whether he has indeed concealed something. A search was done. It appeared there were certain facts concerning which he did fail to speak: verification proved those facts were imagined, p. 582).

By concentrating on the question of Villehardouin's sincerity, both Pauphilet and Faral were battling over psychological issues that were, and are, ultimately unverifiable. Furthermore, an argument over sincerity implies that history is to be evaluated primarily on its factual accuracy and its avoidance of subjectivity – dubious determinants even now, but definitely a *fausse piste* for an era that understood *historia* as history-cum-story. Unquestionably, Villehardouin is a complex author despite the apparent simplicity of *La Conquête de Constantinople*, but the proper understanding of his narrative is not to be found through the application of misleading criteria. Analysis of his quotation practices is, on the other hand, an invaluable aid. This chapter will examine first his self-referencing, then the words he attributes to others through direct speech.

The author has personally experienced his own history and is his own *auctor*. His self-referencing presents itself in five different guises: Geoffrey of Villehardouin, participant in the Fourth Crusade; Geoffrey of Villehardouin, author; I; we; and the book. Thus, when he quotes himself, he speaks with several voices, and the material associated with each is different.[6]

The simplest and largest category comprises the references to Villehardouin in his professional capacity. (Only those references that include his name are considered here. However, his activities were not always singled out from those of the other Crusaders, and he obviously participated in more events than here appear.) Their frequency is justified: Geoffrey of Villehardouin, Marshal of Champagne and Romania, was a prominent leader and negotiator. The following were his activities in those capacities:

JV (among others) took the cross in 1199 (5);[7] JV was named one of the leaders' envoys to Venice (12); JV acted as their spokesman before the doge (27); JV returned direct to France with Alard Maquereau to report on the Franco-Venetian negotiations (32); JV met intending Crusaders as he travelled (33); on arrival in Troyes, JV found his lord Thibaut of Champagne mortally ill (35); after Thibaut's death, JV and three others (named) urged Odo, Duke of Burgundy, to lead the expedition (38); JV reported these unsuccessful negotiations to a Crusading parliament at Soissons (41); JV and Hugh of Saint-Paul were chosen to urge certain leading Crusaders to proceed from Venice rather than by other routes (53); JV was in the fifth division for the siege of Constantinople (151); JV was chosen as one of the four Crusading envoys to deliver an ultimatum to the emperor (211); JV remained with Miles of Brabant and Manasses of Lisle to help Conon of Béthune guard the palaces of Blachernae and Boukoleon (268); JV was asked to go to Adrianople and resolve the differences between the emperor and the marquis (283); JV was well regarded by the marquis and was able to reproach him (285); JV succeeded in urging the marquis in the direction of a negotiated settlement (286); JV and Manasses of Lisle were warmly welcomed on their return by those who wished a settlement (287); JV was elected one of the five envoys to go to the marquis to make peace (296); JV begged the marquis to go to Constantinople for the reconciliation (297); JV was given Demotika in fief by the marquis who had taken it over (299); JV's nephew Joffroi de Villehardouin won the cooperation of a Greek in Modon (325); on the emperor's command JV left Constantinople to consolidate Crusading gains in the surrounding regions (343); JV and Manasses of Lisle were entrusted with guarding the camp at Adrianople while the emperor attacked John of Wallachia (354); after the army's mad pursuit of the enemy, JV was detailed to keep guard on the city side (356); while on guard, JV arrested the flight of the Crusading army (362); at Rodosto, JV consulted the doge about salvaging the desperate situation (364); it was planned that JV would take the rear guard in a night retreat (365); JV did this (366); the doge and JV rode till dawn (369); Count Louis's men joined up with JV, who was leading the rear guard (371); they asked JV's intended strategy (372); JV rode ahead and led them to Carlopolis (373); JV led the vanguard a night and a day to reach Rodosto (374); JV pleaded with deserters to remain and to support the occupation (378); five ship-loads of deserters who had previously agreed to meet JV and the doge left stealthily before the meeting (379); JV's nephew arrived with a company of reinforcements (382); they found the doge and JV at Rodosto and were welcomed by them (384); Henry, the doge, and JV held a meeting (386); JV led the vanguard against John of Wallachia in Demotika (430); JV and others (named) rode to the rescue of Renier of Trit (436); the latter did not recognize JV's vanguard (437); JV dispatched men to investigate (438); Henry sent JV and Miles of Brabant to escort Henry's future wife Agnes (457); JV and others held a brief parley with the emperor concerning those besieged at Cibotos (466); the emperor, JV, and the others decided to attempt a rescue immediately (468); JV and the others manned galleys to rescue Peter of Bracieux and Payen d'Orléans (478); the marquis gave JV Messinople in fief (496).

All of the 51 references above are presented as third-person narrative, and all are independently verifiable. Unquestionably, Villehardouin was a major player in the Fourth Crusade.

When, however, Villehardouin names himself as author, the material he introduces appears subjective, even superfluous, as if his role as author mattered less to him than his active role of negotiator and diplomat. He ends his terse non-description of Constantinople, the "rich city" with its "high walls," "rich towers," "rich palaces," and "high churches" using the inexpressibility topos: "dont il i avoit tant que nuls nel poïst croire se il ne le veïst a l'oil" (there were so many of them that no one could have believed it if he had not seen it with his own eyes, 128). The eyewitness experience that confirmed Villehardouin's authority as historian is not exploited here to confirm his competence as author, for no one could have believed his description unless he too were an eyewitness. (This attempt to grant eyewitness status to his public, inviting them to imagine a dramatic scene, is borrowed from the *chansons de geste*, which regularly invited their listeners through the formula "lors veïssiez" [then you would have seen] to envisage details as if they had been present.)

In two other places, Villehardouin the eyewitness in his authorial role guarantees the material while simultaneously hinting at its inadequacy because it is second- or third-hand oral testimony:

> Et ce tesmoigne Joffrois de Villehardoin li mareschaus de Champaigne, qui ceste ouvre traita, que plus de .XL. li distrent par verité que il virent le confanon Sain Marc de Venise en une des tors et unc ne sorent qui l'i porta (And JV, Marshal of Champagne, who composed this book, bears witness that more than 40 told him that they truly saw the standard of St Mark of Venice on one of the towers and they never learned who carried it there, 174).
>
> Cil qui ceste ystoire traita ne seut s'il fu a tort ou a droit; mes il en oï un chevalier blasmer, qui avoit a nom Ansols de Remi, qui ere hom liges Tyerri de Los le seneschal et chevetaines de sa gent, et le guerpi (The person who composed this book did not learn whether it was rightly or wrongly, but he heard a knight named Anseau de Rémi, liegeman of seneschal Thierry de Los and captain of his men, incur blame for abandoning him, 484).

In the four other instances when the author speaks of himself *qua* author, he uses his name to confirm the unconfirmable or vouches for statements of unverifiable hyperbole or declares the truth of the undiscoverable:

> Et bien testimoigne Joffrois li mareschaus de Champaigne, qui ceste oevre dita, que ainc n'i menti de mot a son escient, si com cil qui a toz les conseils fu, que onc si bele chose ne fu veüe (And J, Marshal of Champagne, who composed this work, and never to the best of his knowledge said an untrue word in it, having been present at all the councils, firmly testifies that never was there such a beautiful sight before, 120).

Et bien tesmoigne Joffrois li mareschaus de Champaigne, qui ceste ovre dita, que onques sor mer ne s'aiderent genz mielz que li Venisien firent (And J, Marshal of Champagne, who composed this work, firmly testifies that no men ever fought better at sea than the Venetians did, 218).

Et bien tesmoigne Joffrois de Vilehardoin li mareschaus de Champaigne, a son escient par verté, que, puis que li siecles fu estorez, ne fu tant gaainié, en une ville (And JV, Marshal of Champagne, who composed this work truthfully to the best of his knowledge, firmly testifies that since the world began there never was such so much booty won in one city, 250).

Et bien tesmoigne Joffrois de Vilehardoin li mareschaus de Romenie et de Campaigne que onc en nul termene ne furent gent si chargié de guerre (And JV, Marshal of Romania and Champagne, who composed this work firmly testifies that never at any moment were men so overburdened with warfare, 460).

His epic hyperbole is never verifiable, but the awe, beauty, and uniqueness of the Fourth Crusade are urged upon the audience with divine omniscience ("never so much plunder since the beginning of the world") coupled with an admission of the inadequacy of his information ("truthfully to the best of his knowledge").

Villehardouin's first-person comments using "je" play a different role in reinforcing material because, between Villehardouin's testimony and the audience's reception of it, there were at least two intermediaries, scribe and (oral) reader. It was through these proxies that Villehardouin addressed the French "seigneurs" from his fief in Romania. Thus the ostensible "je" of "cil Folques dont je vos di" (this Fulk I am telling you about) or "manda par lui le pardon tel con je vos dirai" (proclaimed the indulgence through him, as I am about to tell you) was, for the French audience, *not* Villehardouin the author who participated in these events (cf. para. 120, quoted on p. 42, this volume) but a reader exploited by Villehardouin in anticipation of the oral reading of his history. His "je," a conventional identity by its ambiguity and its formulaic tradition, introduces incomplete or unverifiable data:

Des paroles que li dux dist, bones et belles, ne vos puis tout raconter (Of the fine and beautiful words spoken by the doge I cannot tell you everything, 30).

Je ne vos puis mie toz cels nomer qui a ceste ouvre faire furent (I cannot name all those who worked on this enterprise, 114).

Tolz les cops et tols les bleciez et toz les mors ne vos pui mie raconter (All the blows and all the wounded and all the dead I cannot recount for you, 168).

Et ne sai quex genz por mal mistrent le feu en la ville (I do not know what persons maliciously started a fire in the city, 203).

Ne sai quels genz ... mistrent le feu entr'aus et les Grex (I do not know what persons set a fire between themselves and the Greeks, 247).

Ensi sejornerent ne sai quanz jorz (They remained like this I do not know how many days, 271).

Ne sai comment Esturions le sot (I do not know how Esturion learned of this, 479).

The phrases are deceptively simple, and the *Gesta Francorum* had employed just such a means.[8] The use of this formula in the context of a French vernacular history allows for more possibilities than the "ignoro" of Anonymous:

a) Villehardouin's inability to remember;
b) Villehardouin's unwillingness to report;
c) the scribe's inability to remember;
d) the scribe's unwillingness to report;
e) the oral reader's intervention; or
f) various combinations of the above.

Whatever identities were masked by "je," the fact remains that it served, however formulaically, to suppress portions of frequently controversial material, and it disguised rather than revealed Villehardouin's personal views.

The use of the first-person plural ostensibly encompasses an even wider group than "je": "Or vos lairons de cels qui devant Costantinople sunt, si parlerons de cels qui alerent as autres pors" (Now we shall leave those who are outside Constantinople, and shall speak of those who left for the other ports, 229).

Author, projected reader, projected audience, and even scribe are included in the ill-defined range of personalities who in unison are producing *La Conquête*. As with "je," however, the first-person verb does not imply a personal approach to the material. There is no device more formulaic than the convenient and conventional phrase by which the audience is drawn willy-nilly from one subject to the next.[9] Personal in the sense that it expects – and effects – personal involvement in the narration, it is the least individual of Villehardouin's stylistic techniques.

There is divine impersonality and divine simplicity in the implied imperative of "or lairons."

"The book" is, conversely, a most complex designation. The citation of a written authority by vernacular writers[10] suggested (often erroneously) that they had consulted the most trustworthy sources (i.e., the ancients). But if citation of a written source was valid for and validated a book of fables, such citation in contemporary chronicling seems superfluous. Faral interprets "li livres" simply as "le livre même qu'il composait" (the same book he was writing).[11] If one remembers Villehardouin's necessary anticipation of a reader-narrator, Faral's restrictive explanation is theoretically possible. "Quod scriptum est" (what is written – reader's viewpoint) would thus merge with "quod dixi" (what I have said – Villehardouin's viewpoint) in "li livres" (the book). But should all previous vernacular tradition be disregarded, and the valuable suggestion of "quod scripserunt (auctores)" (what the *auctores* have written) be lost? "Li livres" and its even more suggestive variant "escrit" (writing)[12] are valuable in their ambiguity, especially in problematic contexts like recruitment, fidelity, and sworn agreements, for they imply the coincidence of external authority with personal testimony:

En la terre le conte Thibaut de Campaingne se croisa Garniers li evesques de Troies, li quens Gautiers de Briene ... et maintes hautres bones gens dont li livres ne fait mie mention (In Count Thibaut of Champagne's territory Garnier, Bishop of Troyes, and Count Gautier of Brienne took the cross ... and many other good men of whom the book makes no mention, 5).

Et tant vos retrait li livres que il ne furent que .XII. qui les sairemenz jurerent de la partie des François, ne plus n'en pooient avoir (And the book tells you this much, that there were only 12 from among the Franks who swore the agreements, and they could not get any more, 99).

Je ne vos puis mie toz cels nomer qui a ceste ouvre faire furent ... li livre testimoigne bien que plus de la moitié de l'ost se tenoient a lor acort (I cannot name all those who were part of this effort ... the book testifies that more than half of the army was in agreement with them, 114).

Et cil se defandirent mult bien, et bien tesmoigne li livres que onques a plus grant meschief ne se defendirent .XL. chevalier a tant de gent: et bien i parut, que il n'en i ot mie .V. qui ne fuissent navré de toz les chevaliers qui i estoient (And they defended themselves very well, and the book bears clear witness that never did 40 knights defend themselves against so many with such great loss: and this became clearly apparent, for of all the knights who were there only five were not wounded, 464).

Although in all 17[13] occurrences of "li livres" there is none for which the interpretation of "the book" as *La Conquête* is nonsense, there is also none that would not profit from the added authority, and in some examples (e.g., the passage just cited from 464) there is actually a separation in form between the testimony of the book and what was observed by the eyewitness(es) present: "li livres" versus "et bien i parut."

This examination of the various means by which Villehardouin has disclosed (or disguised!) his identity in *La Conquête* reveals a multivoiced author who owes much to the techniques and ideals of the *chanson de geste*. Other literary quotations, principally scriptural and proverbial, come from a stock of remembered phrases in the mind of this skilled but pragmatic soldier. He does not resort to classical sources but prefers *dicta* of a commonsense variety. The wise man is the one who chooses the right path ("si fait que sages qui se tient devers le mielz," 231); murder will out ("murtres ne puet estre celez," 224); a fed soldier fights better than a hungry one ("plus seürement guerroie cil qui a la vïande que cil qui n'en a point," 131); covetousness is the root of all evil ("covoitise [qui] est racine de toz mals," 253). Such quotations are of course deployed to support the actions of those who are on the right side (i.e., those who tried to fulfil the Crusaders' commitments to the Venetians) and to decry the actions of those in the wrong (i.e., the defectors).

Of all Villehardouin's quotation practices, however, it is his deployment of direct speech that is most revealing. As might be expected, his chronicle shows no trace of Quintilian's conception of history as a genre akin to poetry, a loose sort of song relieving the tediousness of narrative by words remote from common usage, and by the bold employment of figures ("Est enim proxima poetis et quodammodo carmen solutum … et verbis remotioribus et liberioribus figuris narrandi taedium evitat").[14] Villehardouin does not follow the prescriptions of classical rhetoric, which encouraged the historian to use oration for elaborate display and for the imaginative reconstruction of character. Like the author of the *Gesta Francorum*, his preferred model is oral narrative, his stylistic choices have much in common with the *Gesta Francorum*, and his direct speech passages move the narrative forward while dramatizing important points of view. His usage is different from the *Gesta*, however, in that direct speech does not occur uniformly throughout the work.

The most informative *and* the most frequent examples occur in the first 200 paragraphs. The authority of the material in the speeches comes, Villehardouin proudly says, from his presence at all the councils, and their speeches are seen from Villehardouin's vantage point as marshal and chief negotiator. The first cluster of direct speech passages leading to the Franco-Venetian treaty of 1201 stars the doge of Venice, who shares the epic qualities of both Roland and Oliver in that he is both very wise and very courageous: "mult sages et mult proz" (15).

The doge delivers a formal welcome to the envoys (one of whom is Villehardouin), and acknowledges the nobility of the French barons who have sent them: "Seingnor, je ai veües vos letres. Bien avons queneü que vostre seignor sont li plus haut home qui soient sanz corone ..." (My lords, I have seen your letters. We are certainly cognizant of the fact that your lords are the very noblest of the uncrowned ..., 16). The envoys ask that the doge assemble his council so that they may deliver their request: "Sire, nos volons que vos aiez vostre conseil ..." (My lord, we desire that you assemble your council ..., 17). Three days later, in the doge's palace, they speak "en tel maniere" (in this manner – obviously not *ipsissima verba*) to the doge's council: "Sire, nos somes a toi venu de par les hals barons de France qui ont pris le sine de la crois por la honte Jesu Crist vengier et por Jerusalem conquerre, se Diex le vuelt soffrir ..." (My lord, we have come to you on behalf of the noble barons of France who have taken the sign of the cross to avenge the shame done to Jesus Christ and to conquer Jerusalem, if that is God's will ..., 18). A to-and-fro of quick questions ("'En quele maniere?' fait li dux") ("In what way?" says the doge) and answers ("'En totes les manieres,' font li message, 'que vos lor savrez loer ne conseillier que il faire ne soffrir puissent ...'") ("In every way that you will advise or propose to the extent of their abilities," say the messengers) sketch the initial request. The doge remarks on the magnitude of the enterprise ("'Certes,' fait li dux, 'grant chose nos ont requise et bien semble que il beent a halt afaire'"), and asks for eight days to consult ("They have certainly asked for a great thing," says the doge, "and it seems that they are indeed intent on a noble enterprise," 19).

In eight days the envoys return, and the doge delivers his terms in direct speech (20–3), which constitutes Villehardouin's summary of the terms of the *Nolis* treaty of 1201.[15] Villehardouin indicates the abbreviation: "Totes les paroles qui la furent dites et retraites ne vos puis mie raconter" (I cannot recount to you all the words that were spoken and brought forward there, 20); the quotation of a Latin document, short or long, would anyway have been inappropriately tedious for his audience. The envoys depart for their own discussion, find the terms favourable, and return the next day to the doge, who then works with his council to prepare for a full assembly in the Church of St Mark.

Villehardouin, the envoys' spokesman, delivers an 11-line speech, after which, saying they have been instructed not to abandon supplication until their request has been granted, the envoys kneel weeping while the doge and the whole gathering in the Church of St Mark raise their hands upwards and cry out in one voice "Nos l'otrions! Nos l'otrions!" (We agree! We agree!, 28). The collective utterance completes the negotiations that have been so cogently reported in direct speech, and, by giving prominence to the spoken word, Villehardouin formalizes and dramatizes an agreement that will now bind the two parties for better or worse. That is Villehardouin's expectation, at least. When the agreement founders, those Crusaders who chose to leave the expedition become "cil qui l'ost voloient depecier" (those who wanted to break up the expedition). In Villehardouin's view they are more reprehensible than any enemy.

On the controversial issue of the best means to achieve the expedition's ends – whether to obey the leaders' decision and attack Zara or defect and sail directly to Jerusalem – Villehardouin obviously argued for the former. His presentation of the papal interview with the leaders' emissaries in 1203, when the Crusaders ask forgiveness from the pope after the attack, is therefore of some importance. The report contains an intriguing mix of tenses, and a careful blending of direct speech with indirect speech and with free indirect speech. The four Crusading emissaries – Bishop Nivelon of Soissons, John of Noyon, John of Friaise, and Robert of Boves – present the leaders' justification for their attack upon a Christian city, and beg for absolution in direct speech:

> Li baron merci vos crient de la prise de Jadres, que il le fistrent come cil qui mielz ne pooient faire por la defaute de cels qui estoient alé aus autres porz et que autrement ne pooient tenir l'ost ensemble; et sor ce mandent a vos conme a lor bon pere que vos a lor conmandoiz vostre comandement, que il sont prest de faire. (106)

> (The barons beg your forgiveness for the capture of Zara. The reason they did it was that they were unable to do any better because of the defection of those who departed for the other ports. Without doing it, they could not have held the army together. And they send you, their good father, this request that you tell them what you command, for they are ready to obey.)

Their request argues the leaders' point of view, and its presentation in direct speech makes it a dramatic moment in Villehardouin's history.

The pope's response is reported in indirect speech (indirect reporting in several senses, since the words of the Crusading leaders were reported to the pope, the pope's words were reported back to the leaders, and were then reported in *La Conquête de Constantinople* by Villehardouin). Villehardouin's summary does not appear to misrepresent the pope's response in any substantial way, although the tone of that response may have been very different. (In a letter written a year later to the bishop of Soissons, the pope speaks of his sadness over Zara, and of the harsh tone and tough response with which he greeted the envoys.)[16] Villehardouin's reported speech conveys the all-important news that the Crusaders wanted to hear, *viz.*, their absolution. The switches into free indirect speech here are revealing:

> Et li apostoille dist aus messages qu'il savoit bien que por la defaute des autres lor convint a faire, si en ot grant pitié; et lor manda as barons et as pelerins salut et qu'*il les asolt* comme ses filz et lor conmandoit et prioit que il tenissent l'ost ensemble: *car il savoit bien que sanz cele ost ne pooit li servises Dieu estre fais*; et dona plain pooir a Nevelon lo vesque de Soisons et a maistre Johan de Noion de lier et de deslier les pelerins tresqu'adonc que li cardenax vendroit en l'ost. (107; my emphasis)

> (And the pope told the envoys that he was fully aware that they had to do it because of the others' defection, and he was full of regret because of it; he sent his greeting to the barons and to the pilgrims; *he absolves them* as his sons, and ordered and beseeched them to keep the army together: *for he knew of a certainty that without this army God's service could not be done*; and he gave full authority to Nevelon, Bishop of Soissons, and to Master John of Noyon to bond and to unloose the pilgrims until the cardinal came to the army.)

Thus Pope Innocent III is indirectly reported to have granted exactly what the barons wanted as it was formulated by their envoys, and in that report Villehardouin uses free indirect speech to convey two crucial elements: a) the pope's absolution, which is conveyed in a dramatic present tense "il les asolt," as if the pope were uttering "absolvo" (I absolve) in an eternal present moment; and b) the pope's (apparently) unquestioning acceptance of the leaders' argumentation through the ambiguous "car il savoit bien que sanz cele ost ne pooit li servises Dieu estre fais" (for he knew with certainty that without this army God's service could not be done). It is impossible to know whether "car il savoit" represents the pope's own remarks and thoughts, or whether it is Villehardouin's explanation added gratuitously to justify a policy for which he and the other Crusading leaders were responsible. The syntactic ambiguity derives from the flexibility of tense usage in the medieval vernacular and from Villehardouin's well-chosen quotation practices, here, most especially, of free indirect reporting.[17]

Further chosen devices from vernacular rhetoric are used in a persuasive speech by the doge when the army is three leagues away from Constantinople (130–1). He urges the re-victualling of the army before the attack, using a judicious mix of idealistic sententiousness and popular wisdom. First, he establishes his superior competence on the subject. He then reminds the army of the serious magnitude of the enterprise ahead: "Vos avez le plus grant afaire et le plus perillous entrepris que onques genz entrepreïssent" ("You have the greatest mission and the most perilous undertaking that any army ever undertook"). With that *annominatio* of "entrepris"-"entrepreïssent," he stresses the uncertainties and responsibilities of the task ahead, and points to the necessity for prudence in an epic enterprise: "por ce si convendroit que on ovrast sagement" ("it would therefore be advisable to act prudently"). The word "sagement" (wisely) is a cautionary reminder perhaps of the epic disaster of *La Chanson de Roland*, where, it should be remembered, Oliver was "sage" (wise) and Roland was "preux" (brave). Roland's disaster, it was suggested, was precipitated by Roland's lack of *sagesse* (wisdom). Significantly, in *La Conquête de Constantinople*, Villehardouin characterizes the doge as both "sages" *and* "preuz" – "viels hom ere et gote ne veoit, mais mult ere sages et preuz et vigueros" (he was an old man and was totally blind, but he was very wise and brave and vigorous, 364).

When the wise *and* brave doge spells out his advice to the army, Villehardouin stresses the crucial arguments though apostrophe, repetition, and antithesis:[18]

Sachiez, se nos alons a la terre ferme, la terre est granz et large; et nostre gent sont povre et diseteus de la vïande: si s'espandront par la terre por querre la vïande; et il i a mult grant plenté de la gent el païs: si ne porriens tot garder que nos n'en perdissiens; et nos n'avons mestier de perdre, que mult avons poi de gent a ce que nos volons faire. (130)

(Know this, that if we disembark, the territory is large and wide; and our men are poor and starving; and they will scatter to look for food; and there is such an abundant population there that we could not avoid losses; and we must not incur losses, for we have few men for what we want to accomplish.)

Reaching the solution to the army's predicament seemingly fortuitously, the doge then observes that there are Greek islands nearby: "Il a isles ci prés, que vos poez veoir de ci" (There are islands close by, which you can see from here). The repetition of "ci" emphasizes the islands' accessibility. The repeated mention of "blez" and "vïandes" in "isles ... laborees de *blez* et de *vïandes* ... recuillons les *blés* et les *vïandes* ... et quant nos avrons les *vïandes* recuillies, alomes devant la ville et fesons ce que Nostre Sires nos avra porveü" (islands ... producing *corn* and *provisions* ... let us gather the *corn* and *provisions* ... and when we have gathered *provisions*, let us approach the city and do what Our Lord will have intended for us) dangles tantalizing bait. By invoking "Nostre Sires," the doge brings divine planning into the mix, claiming that God's purpose will be better furthered with the doge's plan of re-victualling. God helps those who help themselves or, as he pithily concludes: "Quar plus seürement guerroie cil qui a la vïande que cil qui n'en a point" (A fed soldier is a better soldier than an unfed one, 131).

Slightly[19] longer pieces of oratory are the speeches exchanged between the Greek and the Crusading envoys. The key theme is the crusaders' entry into Greek territory.[20] Both are in direct speech and both are couched in politely elegant terms, beginning with the opening panegyric of the Franks by the Greeks: "Seignor, fait il, l'emperere Alexis vos mande que bien set que vos iestes la meillor gent qui soient sanz corone et de la meillor terre qui soit." This hyperbolic compliment provides a smooth entry into the emperor Alexius's rebuke, which contrasts the present behaviour of the Crusaders with their fine reputation: "et mult se merveille por quoi ne a quoi vos iestes venu" (so he wonders very much for what and to do what you have come). The repetitions in "por quoi ne a quoi" (for what and to do what) and "en sa terre ne en son regne" (in his territory and in his kingdom) emphasize the inappropriateness (in the emperor's view) of the Crusaders' presence. The parallelism of "vos estes crestïen et il est crestïens" (you are Christian and he is Christian) points out that Alexius and the crusaders share a common religion and should not therefore be at odds with each other. "Bien set" (he knows well), which has already been used in the first sentence in Alexius's compliment to the Franks, is a reminder of the professed purpose of this Crusade: "vos iestes meü por la sainte terre d'oltremer et por la sainte croiz et por le sepulcre rescore" (you set out to rescue the Holy Land across the sea and the Holy Cross and the Sepulchre). The invasion of Greek territory is conspicuously absent from that triple anaphora.

"Se vos iestes povres ne disetels, il vos donra volentiers de ses vïandes e de son avoir" (If you are in poverty and need, he will willingly give you some of his provisions) conveys the expansiveness of Alexius's offer to meet the army's hypothetical needs, "povres" reaching resolution with "vïandes," "disetels" with "avoir." (It is worth noting that Alexius uses the same words, i.e., "povre et disetels" and "vïande," as had the doge, when in paragraph 130 he urged the Crusaders to linger/plunder in Greek territory.) The sentence ends starkly with the command "et vos li vuidiez sa terre." "Just get out!" is all the Greek emperor requires in return for his generosity. The change from the attenuation of the conditional verb in "Ne vos voldroit autre mal faire" (He would not otherwise wish to do you harm) with death and defeat to the actuality of the present tense "et ne por quant s'enna il le pooir" (and yet he has the power to do so) is a thinly veiled threat that he proceeds to spell out statistically: "car, se vos estiez .xx. tant de gent, ne vos en porroiz vos aler" (for even if you were 20 times as many in number, if he wished to do you harm, you will not be able to depart). There is similar threat in the change from the hypothetical "estiez" (were) to the direct future verb "porroiz" (will not be able). The potential outcome of the army's actions if it chooses to remain in Constantinople is clear: the death and defeat of "que vos ne fuissiez mort ne desconfit."

Villehardouin enjoys the formulation of the Crusaders' reply, since he introduces it with a complimentary remark on the skill of his fellow-ambassador "qui ere bons chevaliers et sages et bien eloquens" (who was a fine knight, wise and very eloquent). The very eloquent Conon takes up those portions of the emperor's speech that he intends to challenge and render innocuous: "Bels sire, vos nos avez dit que vostre sires se merveille mult por quoi nostre seigneur et nostre baron sont entré en son regne ne en sa terre" (Fine sir, you have told us that your lord wonders very much why our lords and our barons have come to his kingdom and to his land). Rather than shying away from the vexed question of "sa terre" (his land), Conon harps on it, twisting it, however, to his own use. "Sa terre," instead of implying criticism of the Crusaders' right to encroach, now becomes a criticism of Alexius's right to rule. A neat chiasmus emphasizes the point: "por quoi nostre seigneur et nostre baron *sont entré* en son regne ne en sa terre. En son regne ne en sa terre *il ne sont mie entré*; car il le tient a tort ..." (why our lords and our barons have come to his kingdom and to his country. They have not come to his kingdom and to his country; for he possesses it wrongly). It is noteworthy that the possessive adjectives "son" and "sa" (his) carry a heavy stress here. The *emphasis* of Conon's remark would be enhanced for Villehardouin's public when read aloud.

A second chiasmus of thought occurs immediately afterwards, if "a tort" is equivalent to "contre raison" and "a pechié" is equivalent to "contre Dieu." "En son regne ne en sa terre il ne sont mie entré; quar il le tient *a tort* et a pechié contre Dieu et *contre raison*" (They have not come to his kingdom and to his country; for he possesses it wrongly in defiance of God and reason). Although the *annominatio* of "nos li proieriens que il li *perdonast* et li *donast*" (we would entreat him to *pardon* him and *donate* to him) is less effective to the modern ear, tending to weaken the impact of both promised concessions, this stylistic judgment is anachronistic – *annominatio* was an effective emphatic device in the Middle Ages. The final threat to the envoy in "Et se vos por cestui message n'i revenez altre foiz, ne soiez si hardiz que vos plus i revegniez" (And unless you return on account of this message, do not be so bold as to return ever again) ends the forceful speech on an unpleasant note.

The tone of both exchanges is diplomatic but hard-hitting. Their style is studied, not from rich adornment (*amplificatio*), but from stylistic devices suited to the vernacular: emphasis, alliteration, *annominatio*, apostrophe, antithesis, chiasmus, hyperbole, and repetition – especially anaphora. The number of opening conjunctions is drastically reduced and, although the label *disiunctum* would be an exaggeration, the change from the polysyndeton of the narrative is quite marked. Direct speech is always discretionary, after all.

It is enlightening to examine the contexts where Villehardouin chooses to narrate directly in this fashion. The distribution of direct speech passages is one of the more curious features of *La Conquête de Constantinople*. In the first hundred paragraphs, direct speech occurs in thirty-four, in the second hundred it occurs in sixteen, in the third hundred in six, and in the fourth hundred in three. In an essay on direct speech in Villehardouin, Jean Frappier[21] claimed that, given two opposing sides, Villehardouin reserves direct speech for those with whom he agrees, instancing paragraphs 95–6, where the views of the abbé de Vaux (who opposed the Constantinople expedition) are expressed only in indirect speech.[22] He also suggested (albeit cautiously) that the supremacy of indirect narration in the second half of *La Conquête de*

Constantinople reflects an evolution in Villehardouin towards objectivity, "la démarche d'un véritable historien" (the progress of a true historian, ibid., p. 49).

While it is true that the use of direct speech is discretionary for Villehardouin as for our other historians, its variable deployment should be regarded as a valuable indicator of the historians' point of view (in Villehardouin's case, the point of view of a leader and negotiator "who was present at all the councils"), not necessarily as suppression or perversion of the facts.[23] Frappier's desire to see Villehardouin conform to modern expectations, even making him evolve into a modern historian before our eyes, is just one more example of misguided anachronism, and the reduction of dramatic presentation in the second half of the work does not derive from any increase in Villehardouin's capacity to dominate events. That capacity was obvious from the beginning. Nor does the choice of direct as opposed to indirect speech vitiate the content. Queller observes:

> Where Villehardouin's account can be checked against official documents ... he proves to be relatively accurate and quite specific, if somewhat superficial. His description of the negotiations at Venice in early 1201 can be verified in considerable detail by the treaty itself and other official documents ... the tone and style of certain passages, moreover, particularly those recounting the speeches of the envoys, suggest he was working with documents or notes in hand.[24]

The reasons for this decrease in Villehardouin's use of direct speech are to be found elsewhere, *viz.*, from a change in direction of the events themselves and from a consequent change in Villehardouin's attitude to them. Villehardouin had validated his eyewitness authority in terms of his participation in the councils, as "cil qui a toz les conseils fu." That was his area of expertise and the source of his pride. During the desperate task to hold on to the diminishing number of Crusading strongholds in Romania, dramatic moments were decreasing, as was his ability to influence events. The difficulties of the Crusading army, scattered over a territory where the only possibility now was to hold on to isolated fortresses, undermined Villehardouin's epic vision, and with it his epic presentation of events. The last truly epic utterance came from the mortally wounded Count Louis of Blois who, when urged by some of his retainers to leave the battle, echoed Count Roland when *he* faced overwhelming odds: "Ne place Dam le Dieu que ja més me soit reprové que je fuie de camp et laise l'empereor" (May the Lord God forbid that I ever be reproached for fleeing the battle-field and abandoning the emperor, 359).

The few remaining instances of direct speech in the later part of the work reflect the dire circumstances and dwindling hopes of the Crusaders. Most of them record pleas for help. Villehardouin asks the doge to lead a rescue expedition after the deaths of the Emperor Baldwin and Count Louis (364). Those surviving the battle at Adrianople request help from Villehardouin, who heads a rear guard to lead them to safety (372). A group of French supporters in Philippopolis lose heart and ask help from the Bulgars (399), but Greeks in Demotika who had turned to Johannitza challenge him (425), then messengers from Adrianople plead with the emperor's brother Henry to help both them and Demotika (428). Henry takes counsel and is told: "Seignor, nus somes ja tant venu avant, que nos somes honi se nos ne seccorons le Dimot: mais soit chascun confés et conmemié, et ordenons nos batailles" (My lord barons, we have already come so far that we are shamed if we do not rescue Demotika; let every man take confession and be shriven, then let us get the battalions into formation, 429). The warriors fall silent in the remaining 71 paragraphs, and the chronicle ends with the decapitation of Villehardouin's hero, the marquis Boniface de Montferrat, whose head is sent to Johannitza. "This tragedy happened in the year of Our Lord 1206" (500).

The beginning of the work had been alive with idealism and dramatic in conception. The negotiation sessions in Venice and the assembling of the fleet were among Villehardouin's most vivid memories, eliciting unusual expressions of emotion even from this seasoned military leader (second in rank only to the counts of Blois, Flanders, and Saint Pol). But with the defections and defeats came an increasing pessimism, until Villehardouin eventually commented (460), "onc en nul termene ne furent gent si chargié de guerre, por ce que il estoient espars en tant leus" (never at any time were men so burdened with war because they were dispersed in so many locations).

It is impossible to know whether with hindsight Villehardouin regretted the Crusade's diversion to Constantinople. His overall presentation of events suggests that he did not. In his view, an epic undertaking with epic heroes (among them the doge) and epic traitors (those who refused to follow their leaders), could have been a lived epic but instead turned into an epic tragedy. Unfortunately, his epic presentation now makes both his words and his silences more suspect than those of the lesser-ranking, less informed Robert de Clari: Villehardouin was influential in what was essentially a baronial Crusade, while Robert was the voice of the "underdog."

Why did Villehardouin not discuss in a prologue his reasons for writing *La Conquête de Constantinople*?[25] Why did he not provide more details of the doge of Venice's hard bargaining, of the pope's interdiction forbidding an attack upon Christian cities, or of the doge's alleged defiance of the pope?[26] Why does his narrative end abruptly with the death of the marquis Boniface de Montferrat? And – the ultimate silence – why do we hear nothing of Villehardouin's whereabouts and activities after that, so that the place and circumstances of his death (between 1212 and ca. 1218) remain a mystery to this day?

Queller and colleagues point out in an article on those (should one call them "the silent majority"?) who did not participate in the conquest of the Byzantine capital or did so unwillingly[27] that many historians do not accept Villehardouin's condemnation of these defectors. Some go further and indict Villehardouin as a dishonest historian, although, according to Queller, "it is with justice that Villehardouin points out that those who insisted on going directly to the Holy Land failed to accomplish anything against the infidel" (p. 465). Thus anachronistic expectations continue to fuel modern judgments of what Villehardouin *should* and *should not* have said. However, Villehardouin's practices of quotation *and* his silences stem from his personal conception of the Fourth Crusade as an epic *manqué*. For him, the tragedy was that things could have been otherwise, and nothing conveys the dwindling of his epic enthusiasm better than his quotation practices as he tells *his* history/story of *La Conquête de Constantinople*.

Chapter Four

In the Words of the Poor Knight Robert de Clari

La Conquête de Constantinople

Like Villehardouin, Robert de Clari was a participant in the Fourth Crusade, but the two Crusaders could not have been more different. Robert identified with the army's *povres chevaliers* (poor knights); was not present at any of the councils; had no inside knowledge of the leaders' deliberations; and claimed no particular authority. He was the son of Gilon de Clari (Cléry),[1] inhabited a fiefdom to the northwest of Amiens, and followed his suzerain Pierre d'Amiens throughout the Crusade until the conquest of Constantinople, returning to France before the Crusade unravelled. It is clear from his narrative that he did not take part in the retreat from Adrianople in April 1205. He is presumed to have been the "Robilardus" of the inscription on a reliquary in the abbey of Corbie: "Bene sit Robilardo qui me attulit Constantinopoli" [Blessed be Robilard who brought me from Constantinople],[2] where he gifted relics from Constantinople's Great Palace (Boukoleon) on his return to France. He mentions the death of the emperor Henry in paragraph CXIX, and must still have been living, therefore, in June 1216. Beyond that we have no further information and although *La Conquête de Constantinople*[3] constitutes his Crusading memoirs,[4] there are only two places where Robert de Clari actually inserts his name.

The first is during an account of the prowess of his brother, Aleaumes, during the capture of the tower of Galata in 1204. Aleaumes had been introduced at the beginning of the work as "Aleaumes de Clari en Aminois li clers, qui mult y fu preus et molt y fist de hardement et de proesches" (Aleaumes de Clari the Amiens cleric, who was very courageous in the Crusade and performed many acts of bravery and prowess, para. I, lines 87–9). Robert subsequently claims that Aleaumes performed more acts of physical courage than any other man in the army, with the exception of Pierre de Bracheux (para. LXXVI, lines 15–20), and provides specifics in the next paragraph. When the Crusaders are picking away at the Galata postern, Aleaumes sees that no one dared to enter and leaps forward himself, only to be pulled back by his brother: "Si avoit illuec un chevalier, un sien frere, Robers de Clari avoit a non, qui li desfendi et qui dist qu'il n'i enterroit mie; et li clers dist que si feroit, si se met⁵ ens a piés et a mains; et quant ses freres vit chou, si le prent par le pié, si commenche a sakier a lui, et tant que maugré sen frere, vausist ou ne dengnast, que li clers i entra" (And a knight, his brother called Robert de Clari, was there, and he forbade him from entering; and the *clerc* said he would. He gets down on his hands and knees; and when his brother saw that, he grabs him by the foot and begins to pull him back to the point where finally, despite his brother, whether he wished or not, the *clerc* got in, para. LXXVI, lines 2–9).

In this real-life dispute between a *clerc* and a *chevalier*, the courageous *clerc* Aleaumes triumphs unequivocally and the modest *chevalier* Robert seems to mock his own timidity. It is certainly not for personal kudos that he provides his name here.

The other occurrence of his name is in the final paragraph, when he signs off from his history. It was an obvious place for self-congratulation or at least self-justification, but just as Robert was uninterested in *captatio benevolentiae* (striving for goodwill) at the beginning of his work, he is now uninterested in pleading for indulgence at its conclusion. He says simply:

> Ore avés oï le verité, confaitement Coustantinoble fu conquise, et confaitement li cuens de Flandres Bauduins en fu empereres, et mesires Henris ses freres aprés, que chis qui i fu et qui le vit et qui l'oï le tesmongne, ROBERS DE CLARI, li chevaliers, et a fait metre en escrit le verité, si comme ele fu conquise; et ja soit chou que il ne l'ait si belement contee le conqueste, comme maint boin diteur l'eussent contee, si en a il toutes eures le droite verité contee, et assés de verités en a teutes qu'il ne peut mie toutes ramembrer. (para. CXX, lines 1–11)

> (Now you have heard the truth of how Constantinople was conquered, and how Count Baldwin of Flanders became emperor of it, and after him my lord Henry his brother, for that same Robert of Clari who was there and saw it and heard it bears witness to it, and he has had the truth of it put into writing, how it was conquered; and although he may not have narrated the conquest as beautifully as many good storytellers would

have told it, he has nevertheless told the direct truth of it, and there are so many true things pertaining to it that he is unable to recall them all.)

Thus, courting no recognition from posterity and downplaying his narrative skills, Robert turns his final address to his audience into a semi-apology. Compared with Villehardouin's practices, Robert's self-referencing is stark.

Villehardouin's self-naming was of course natural and justifiable when it occurred in the narration of the events in which he played a major role. When, however, it guaranteed hyperbolic statements or confirmed the unconfirmable, it was a different matter. A confident guarantee from Geoffrey of Villehardouin, Marshal of Champagne and (later) Romania, attested to the miraculous appearance ("reported by more than 40 people") of the Venetian standard on a tower; to the report ("according to what someone said") that Ansols de Rémi deserted his overlord; and to the amount of booty ("more than from any city since the world began") garnered in Constantinople. What weight could a similar guarantee carry if "Robers de Clari, povres chevaliers, tes-moingne …" (Robert of Clari, poor knight, bears witness that …)?

While Robert's self-referencing differs substantially from Villehardouin's, the two chroniclers share other narrative assumptions. Their histories anticipate intermediaries between dictation and delivery, and their frequent deployment of first-person pronouns was a convenient – and conventional – way of ordering material for such a context. Villehardouin generally uses "je" either to abbreviate ("I cannot report all the fine words spoken by the doge of Venice"; "I cannot record all the fine blows struck in the battle") or to introduce the unverifiable ("I do not know who set fire to Constantinople"). Robert generally uses "je"[6] in anticipatory fashion to move the narrative forward, or, in recapitulatory mode, to remind his listeners of what has gone before.

The first-person plural is used similarly in phrases that are part of a well-used stock of formulae with which an oral audience would be totally familiar: "we shall now tell you …," "we shall name for you …," "we do not know the number of …," "we cannot tell you …," "we shall leave them for the moment and tell you about …," "we spoke of them before …," "we shall speak of them later …" Its frequency is similar to that of "je."[7] "Nous" also abbreviates what "we" are unable to name, as in "nous ne vous savons tous nommer" (we cannot name them all for you) or "nous n'en savons le nombre" (we do not know their number). These are conventional phrases, and in Robert's history there seems even to be no difference between "je" and "nous." If one were to attempt to draw any conclusion, one might suggest a close teamwork between author and scribe in the dictation process so that no differentiation was necessary.

There are a few exceptions, however. In the narration of *clerc* Aleaumes's daring push into the tower of Galata on his hands and knees with soldier-brother Robert clutching at his foot to pull him back (see this volume, pp. 57–58), the singular and plural pronouns are used within a line of each other, perhaps denoting a separation of identities: "Aliaumes de Clari, li clers, dont *je* vous ai parlé devant, qui si i fu preus de sen cors et qui i fist tant d'armes, comme *nous* vous avons dit par devant" (The cleric Aliaumes de Clari about whom *I* have spoken to you before, who was physically so brave there and who performed so many feats of arms, as *we* have said above, para. XCVIII, lines 8–11; my emphasis). One wonders whether the unusual distinction between "je" and "nos" has any significance. Did brother Aleaumes work in conjunction with Robert and his scribe on this episode, thus making "nos" stand here for three people? (Is it possible even that the literate Aleaumes, a convenient scribe for a poor illiterate knight, might have collaborated with his brother throughout the work? Further hypothesizing would be dangerous without evidence.)

Another juxtaposition of "je" and "nous" occurs during Robert's attempt to convey to his stay-at-home French audience Constantinople's incredible wealth, which neither "I," "we," "any storyteller," "one," nor "any mortal man who ever lived in Constantinople" – in fact, "no one" – can adequately describe. After this accumulation of narratively challenged identities, Robert tells his audience that they would never believe any of these people anyway, thus effectively inviting them to add *their* imagination to the process:

Toutes ches mervelles que *je* vous ai chi acontées, et encore assés plus que *nous* ne vous *poons* mie aconter, trouverent li Franchois en Constantinoble … ne *je* ne quit mie, *par le mien ensient*, que *nus hons conterres* peust nombrer mie toutes les abaïes de le chité … et si nombroit *on* qu'il avoit bien largement en le chité .xxx. m. prestres, que moines que autres. Des autres Grius, des haus, des bas, de pauvres, de riches, de le grandeur de le vile, des palais, des autres mervelles qui i sont vous *lairons nous* ester a dire; car *nus hons terriens*, qui tant eust mes en le chité, ne le vous porroit nombrer ne aconter, que *qui* vous en conteroit le chentisme part de le riqueche ..., sanleroit il que che fust menchoingne, ne ne cresriés vous mie. (para. XCII, lines 24–43; my emphasis)

(In Constantinople the French discovered all these marvels of which *I* have told you here, as well as many more that *we* cannot relate to you ... *I* do not think, to the best of *my* knowledge, that *any narrator* could enumerate all the abbeys of that city ... and *one* estimated that in the city there were a full thirty thousand priests, monks and others. *We* shall give up telling you about the other Greeks, high and low, poor and rich, the grandeur of the town, the palaces, the other marvels that are there; for *no mortal man* who had ever resided in the city could number or tell you them, for if *anyone* were to tell you one hundredth part of the wealth ..., it would seem to be a lie, you would not believe it.)

One final use of a first-person plural verb deserves comment. After reporting the furious outrage of the knights and young *bacheliers* when they heard of unjust distribution of Constantinople's wealth in their absence, Robert interrupts his customarily chronological[8] narration with "Or aviemes evlié a conter une aventure qu'il avint a monseigneur Pierrom de Braiechoel" (Now we had forgotten to tell you of an adventure that happened to my lord Pierre of Bracheux, para. CVI, lines 1–2). The "adventure" that "we" belatedly remembered stars the much-admired Pierre de Bracheux who, when guarding Constantinople during the absence of the new emperor Henry, proudly declared to the would-be invader John of Wallachia and the Comans that Troy had once belonged to "our ancestors." "'Ba!' fist mesires Pierres, 'Troies fu a nos anchiseurs, et chil qui en escaperent si s'en vinrent manoir la dont nous sommes venu; et pour che que fu a nos anchiseurs, sommes nous chi venu conquerre terre'" ("Bah!" said my lord Pierre, "Troy belonged to our ancestors, and those who escaped from it came to live in the place we come from; and because it belonged to our ancestors, we have come here to conquer land"). The Trojan origin of the Franks was a familiar legend in the Frankish army and is one of Robert's rare references to any literary tradition outside the *contes à rire*.[9] Presented here as justification for the Constantinople enterprise, it implies no dependence on a specific source, however, and tells us little about Robert's literary background.

He was not a "bookish" writer. He uses no epic quotations and no epic allusions.[10] He does not attempt, like Villehardouin, to validate his history by citing "li livres." There are no Latin quotations (although he provides an interesting detail about the usage of the Latin hymn "Veni creator spiritus" (Come Creator Spirit),[11] which, he says, the pilgrims asked the priests and clergy to chant from the poops of the ships as the Crusading fleet left Venice harbour, "[e]t trestout et grant et petit plorerent de pec et de le grant goie qu'i eurent" ([a]nd all, great and small, wept with emotion for the great joy they experienced at that moment, para. XIII, lines 30–32).

There are no untranslated quotations from other languages. Nor would they serve any purpose for Robert's French audience. The black king of Nubia, who, Robert notes with interest, has completely black skin and a cross branded with a branding iron on his forehead, expresses his intention to go on pilgrimage through a "latimiers" (interpreter). The exotic foreigner's adventures are recounted to the barons in indirect speech (para. LIV, lines 15–32). Jesus talks to a Constantinople holy man in the French vernacular: "Cha donne … chele toaile" (give me … that towel, para. LXXXIII, lines 12–13) when he imprints a healing image on it. The inscription on Constantinople's Golden Mantle Gate globe reads in Robert's version of it as "tout chil … qui mainent en Constantinoble un an, doivent avoir mantel d'or aussi comme jou ai" (all those … who live in Constantinople for a year are destined to have a golden mantle just like mine, para. LXXXVIII, lines 9–11); and the warnings on the two copper statues in the same city become "De vers Occident venront chil qui Constantinoble conquerront" (From the West will come those who will conquer Constantinople) and "Ichi les boutera on" (Here is where they will be thrown) (para. XCI, lines 7–10). Robert's information about all the marvels of Constantinople was presumably conveyed by a travel guide, but, whatever the source, the manner in which Robert conveyed them would surely not have changed. The content was all important, as was Robert's skill in the telling of it for a French audience.

His enthusiasm for a good story makes him depart occasionally from chronology, for example when he cannot refrain from telling an "adventure" of Pierre de Bracheux's that he had previously forgotten (see p. 61, this volume). Pierre's feisty speech to his alien challengers is just one of many direct speech passages in which the stylistic influence of the *fabliau* and of the *Roman de Renart* (octosyllabic versification aside) is visible.[12] Bourgeois realism also dominates the direct speech passages of a wide range of personages, from Jesus to an innkeeper's wife; from the doge of Venice to the knights and young *bacheliers* in the army; from the marquis of Montferrat, several Greek emperors, and a bishop to an old man in Constantinople – Robert has, in fact, a cast of thousands.[13]

It is the direct speech passages of the doge of Venice that dominate the direction of Robert's narrative, however. The doge looms head and shoulders above everyone, a master of ceremonies who negotiates, proposes, leads, inspires, settles disputes, threatens emperors, and even cocks a snook at the pope. This unwavering respect for Dandolo from both our French chroniclers of the Fourth Crusade is striking. Their portraiture of him – an epic hero for Villehardouin, a "molt preudons" (very worthy man) for Robert – reveals that neither chronicler viewed the diversion of the Crusade away from Jerusalem as a longstanding plot hatched by villainous Venetians. As Queller says in his review of Nada Patrone's edition of *La Conquista di Costantinopoli*:

> I disagree with Nada Patrone's treasonist view of the Fourth Crusade … Like other treasonists, she is indignant that conniving barons and Venetians led the purehearted masses to attack the Eastern Christian capital. Yet peripheral expeditions by crusaders were commonplace, and Christians were often the victims. Those Fourth Crusaders who abandoned the army to go directly to the Levant engaged in war among Christians there while waiting for the truce with the Muslims to end. Even the pope, in his letter allowing the crusaders to associate with the excommunicated Venetians, authorized them to seize food in the Byzantine Empire if Alexius III refused to provide it willingly.[14]

Robert's direct speech representations of the doge's political stances are often feisty. Dandolo's disregard for papal directives concerning Zara is boldly dramatized in this defiant challenge to the papal interdiction:

> Or savoient il bien chil de Jadres que chil de Venice les haoient. Si avoient pourcachié unes lettres de Rome, que trestout chil qui les werieroient ou qui leur feroient nul damage, qu'il fussent eskemenié. Si envoierent ches letres par boins messages au duc et as pelerins qui illueques estoient arivé. Quant li message vinrent a l'ost, si lut on les letres devant le duc et devant les pelerins. Quant les letres furent lutes et li dux les eut entendues, il dist qu'il ne lairoit mie pour l'eskemeniement l'apostoile qu'il ne se venjast de chiax de le vile. A tant s'en alerent li message. Li dux parla autre fois as barons, si leur dist; "Seigneur, sachiés que je ne le lairoie a nul fuer que je ne m'en venjaisse d'aus, ne pour l'apostoile!" (para. XIV, lines 12–26)

(Now the inhabitants of Zara were well aware of the Venetians' animosity. So they had obtained a letter from Rome stating that all who made war on them or harmed them in any way would be excommunicated. And they sent this letter via good messengers to the doge and the Crusaders who had arrived there. When the messengers came to the army, the letter was read in the presence of the doge and the Crusaders. When the letter had been read and the doge had heard it,[15] he said the papal excommunication would not make him refrain from exacting vengeance on the town's citizens. Then the messengers departed. The doge spoke a second time to the leaders and said: "My lords, be assured that, whatever the cost, I would not fail to take vengeance on them, even for the pope.")

It is the doge who prevails again in the argument over the diversion of the expedition to Constantinople. All points of view are neatly, if simplistically, dramatized in the following direct speech summaries, the doge arguing for Alexius's dynastic entitlement to Constantinople; some Crusaders arguing that diversion to Constantinople was not the original purpose of the Crusade; and other Crusaders arguing pragmatically that nothing could be achieved while food and money were lacking:

> "Seigneur," fist li dux, "or avons nous raisnauvle acoison d'aler en Coustantinoble, se vous le loés; car nous avons le droit oïr." Or y eut il aucuns qui ne s'acorderent mie a aler en Coustantinoble, ains disoient: "Ba! que ferons nous en Coustantinoble? Nous avons no pelerinage a faire et ausi pourposement d'aler en Babyloine ou en Alexandre, et no navies ne nous doit sivir que un an et ja est la moitiés de l'anee passee!" Et li autre disoient encontre, "Que ferons nous en Babyloine ne en Alixandre, quant nous n'avons viande ne avoir par coi nous y puissons aler? Miex nous vient il, anchois que nous y aillons, que nous conquestons viande et avoir par raisnavle acoison, que nous y aillons pour morir de fain. Adont si porrons forfaire, et il nous offre a venir avec nous et a tenir no navie et nostre estore encore un an a sen coust!" (para. XXXIII, lines 3–20)

("My lords," said the doge, "we now have a logical reason to go to Constantinople if you advise it, for we have the rightful heir." Now there were some who did not agree to the Constantinople journey, saying, "Bah! What shall we be doing in Constantinople? We have our pilgrimage to make and also a plan to go to Babylon or Alexandria, and our fleet is supposed to follow us for only one year, and half of that year is already over!"

The others argued against this. "What shall we be doing in Babylon or Alexandria when we have no provisions or money to enable the journey? A better plan is to obtain provisions and money because of a good cause than to go there and die of hunger. Then we shall achieve something, and he offers to come with us, and maintain our navy and fleet for one more year at his expense.")

An additional reason, Boniface's personal desire for personal vengeance on the Greeks,[16] is then reported briefly in indirect speech, although it is the doge's pragmatic reasoning that carries the day.

It is noteworthy that despite variations in the context, presentation, and dramatic tone of the doge's speeches, Robert (like Villehardouin) never wavers from his unswerving admiration for the Venetian leader. One presumes that the Venetians shared this adulation of their leader, but did they share the doge's defiant stance vis-à-vis Rome? Might they even have been ignorant of the papal ban, believing themselves to be loyal defenders of the faith? In his recent article "The Venetian Version of the Fourth Crusade: Memory and the Conquest of Constantinople in Medieval Venice," Thomas F. Madden argues for this possibility, and while it seems unlikely that a papal ban known to a rank-and-file Crusader like Robert would escape the notice of the Franks' all-important allies, Madden reminds us that there was minimal interaction between Franks and Venetians, not to mention a language barrier between them. Madden's scholarly reconstruction of Venetian memories from *non*-textual sources suggests that "[l]ike other medieval Europeans, the Venetians were proud of their Crusading victories, not merely as evidence of military prowess, but as a visible indication of the favor God showed to those who defended his people and church."[17] Madden concludes that Venetian and other Italian Crusaders believed that the pope himself had directed the Crusade to Constantinople. The earliest Venetian chronicles of the Crusade (written well after the event and unsatisfactory in many respects) give no hint of the pope's displeasure that his Crusade had been waylaid by "thieves."[18] And since there was no Venetian Villehardouin or Robert de Clari to provide a contemporary record of the Venetian perspective, it was not until the fourteenth century that Venetian narratives of the Fourth Crusade began to reflect the same factual information as the narratives in French, German, Roman, and Byzantine sources.

Dandolo's direct address to his erstwhile Greek ally is no less feisty. From a galley he personally[19] reprimands Alexius for breaking faith with the Crusading army and, after a lively exchange in which the doge remonstrates with the Greek emperor and Alexius refuses to comply, the doge resorts to the language of the gutter to get his message across:

"Alexe, que cuides tu faire?" fist li dux, "preng warde que nous t'avons geté de grant caitiveté, si t'avons fait seigneur et coroné a empereur; ne nous tenras tu mie," fist li dux, "nos convenenches, ne si n'en feras plus?" – "Naie," fist li empereres, je n'en ferai plus que fait en ai! – "Non? ... garchons malvais; nous t'avons," fist li dux, "geté de le merde et en le merde te remeterons; et je te desfi et bien saches tu que je te pourcacherai mal a men pooir de ches pas en avant." (para. LIX, lines 22–31)

"Alexius, what do you think you're doing?" said the doge, "Remember that we got you out of the depths of wretchedness, made you lord, and crowned you emperor; won't you keep your agreement with us, won't you do any more with this?" – "No," said the emperor, "I will do no more than I have already done!" – "No?" ... "You rotten boy," said the doge; "we have dragged you out of the shit, and we will throw you back into the shit; I defy you, and you can be sure of this, I will do my utmost to load all the harm I can onto you from this moment onward.")

In Robert's *fabliau*-style narration, the attitudes of other personages are crystallized in the same direct manner, their characterization often verging on caricature. Emperor Manuel's pro-Latin stance is conveyed through a series of exchanges with the Greeks, the French, and his advisors, which Manuel concludes with a firm (and, surely, audience-pleasing!) declaration of his love for the French: "Mais or kemanch jou, que nus de vous ne soit si osés ne si hardis qu'il ja mais paraut de me largueche, ne de chou que j'aim les Franchois, car je les aim et si me fi plus en aus que en vous; et si leur donrai plus que jou ne leur ai donné" (But now I order that none of you be so bold and presumptuous as to talk to me ever again about my generosity or about my love for the French, for I love them and trust them more than you; and I shall give them more than I have already given them, para. XVIII, lines 74–78).

Robert's public would have been delighted also by his lively narration (abbreviated here) of young Isaac II's adventures before the Crusaders rescued him: Isaac, poverty stricken, hides from Andronicus in a widow woman's house in Constantinople; she lies to Andronicus's steward at her door, "Ha! Sire, pour Dieu merchi! il n'a nul homme chaiens muchié" (Oh, my lord, for the love of God! No man is hidden here, para. XXI, lines 70–1); the steward threatens young Isaac when he emerges, "Ribaus puans, on vous pendera ja!" (Stinking piece of shit, now you'll be hanged, ibid., lines 86–7); Isaac slices through the steward's head with his sword and runs through the street crying, "Seignor, pour Dieu merci, ne me tués mie, car je ai ochis le diable ..." (My lords, in God's name do not kill me, for I have killed the devil ..., para. XXII, lines 10–12); the Greeks rally round him, saying, "Faisons le bien! Faisons de chest vaslet empereur!" (Let's do the right thing! Let's make this boy the emperor, ibid., lines 26–7); the Patriarch says no, "... Se jou le coroune, li empereres Andromes me tueroit et decoperoit tout en pieches" (if I crown him, the emperor Andronicus would kill me and cut me all to pieces, ibid., lines 34–5); but the Greeks tell the Patriarch they will cut off his head unless he obeys. Isaac is crowned emperor by the will of the people. Andronicus, on the other hand, is forced to flee, gets shipwrecked, hides in an innkeeper's house, is discovered (in his imperial robes!), and is confronted with his crimes by Isaac (to whom he say "Taissiés vous ... que je ne vous en dengneroie respondre!"; Shut up ... I would not stoop to giving you an answer, para. XXV, lines 48–50).

Reflecting the amusingly cynical values of a *fabliau*, a characteristic *fabliau* ending of *le trompeur trompé* (the trickster tricked) inevitably follows. Justice is served on Andronicus after much street debate over a suitable punishment for him because of these judicious words from "un sage homme" (a wise man):

Seigneur, se vous me voliés croire, je vous enseingneroie comment nous nous porriemes trop bien vengier de lui. Je ai un camoel en maison, qui est le plus orde beste et le plus foireuse et le plus laide du siecle. Nous prenderons Andromes, si le despoullerons trestout nu, si le loierons au dos du camoel si que ses visages li iert droit ens u cul; si le mesrons d'un kief de le vile dusques a l'autre. Si se porront adonques bien vengier tot chil et toutes cheles a qui il a mesfait. (para. XXV, lines 64–73)

(My lords, if you would trust me, I could tell you how we could avenge ourselves really well. I have a camel at home, the filthiest, vilest, ugliest beast on earth. We'll take Andronicus, strip him naked, and tie him on the back of the camel so that his face is right up its arse: then we'll lead him from one end of the city to the other. That way all the men and women he has wronged will be well avenged.)

The wise man's words carry the day, Andronicus is led through the city on a camel, assaulted at every step with "Vous pendistes men pere, et si geustes a me femme a forche" (ibid., lines 78–80) (you hanged my father, and you raped my wife) until there is no flesh left on his body. His stripped bones are then thrown in a sewer, and the church doors in Constantinople later sport a portrait of Isaac being crowned emperor by a miracle, with Jesus and Mary on either side of him.

Robert's narration of Greek coronation, Greek corruption, and Greek punishment, enlivened by the direct exchanges exemplified above, obviously differs markedly from Villehardouin's in several insubstantial respects. A "bons conterres" (good storyteller) despite his modesty on the subject, Robert produced a sparkling narrative from his experience of the Fourth Crusade. The marshal of Romania, weighed down with leadership responsibilities and disappointments, produced a sober narrative of the plans and perils of "the greatest mission and the most perilous undertaking any army ever undertook." If medieval *historia* was ambiguous by its double connotation of history/story, Robert inclined to the latter while Villehardouin inclined to the former, but factually their histories are never far apart. For their individual "takes" upon those facts, an essential source of information for us now is their deployment of quotation.

Chapter Five

In the Words of the Author

Li Fet des Romains: The Gallic War

Twelve hundred and seventy-one years after Julius Caesar entered Gaul to conquer it for Rome, he was re-introduced to the territory by an anonymous cleric who brought together and translated all known works pertaining to the Roman conqueror in a compilation entitled *Li Fet des Romains*. The compiler says he intends the work to be a history of Rome's 12 emperors, obviously after the model of Suetonius's *Vitae Caesarum*.[1] No subsequent books appeared, however, and later scribes sometimes therefore changed its title from *Li Fet des Romains* to *Li Livre de Julius Cesar* or another such appropriate title.

The date of this first work of classical historiography in the French vernacular can be determined with precision, thanks to several personal remarks from the translator to his public. The first is an explanatory comment about "Lutetia," that is, Paris, which he obviously knows intimately:

Titus Labienus fu venuz devant Lutece, une des citez principax de France, que l'en apele ore Paris; mes n'estoit pas a icel tens de si grant renomee come ele est ore. Quatre legions avoit Labienus o soi. La citez seoit en un isle en mi Saine, si come ele fet anquore, et estoient les entrees mout boeuses. Por ice avoit ele non Lutecia, qui sone "boeuse." Entor le mont Seint Estiene et Seinte Genevieve n'avoit lors nul habitant; mes au tens Seinte Crehelt, qui fonda le mostier dou mon < t > en honor de Seint Pierre l'apostre, ou Flodoveus ses barons gist, i conmença l'en < a > habiter et meesmement puis que li rois Chilperiz, qui fu fiuz de lor fill, ot fet un theaitre es vignes qui or sont entre Seinte Genevieve et Seint Victor. De ce theaitre duroit encore une partie en estant au jor que li rois Phelipe < ·s > conmença Paris a ceindre de mur par devers Petit Pont. (p. 274, lines 17–31)

(Titus Labienus had arrived outside Lutetia, oné of the main French cities, now called Paris; but it was not as famous then as it is now. Labienus had four legions with him. The city was situated in the middle of the Seine, as it is now, and its approaches were very muddy. For this reason it was called Lutetia, which means "muddy city." At the time there were no inhabitants around Mont St Etienne and Sainte Genevieve; but in the time of Saint Clotilda, who founded the Church on the Mount in honour of Saint Peter the Apostle, where her husband Chlovis now lies, habitation began, and similarly, after king Chilperic, son of their son, had built a theatre in the vineyards which now lie between Sainte Genevieve and Saint Victor. Part of this theatre was still standing on the day when King Philip began to wall in Paris over by the Petit Pont.)

The mention of Philip Augustus's fortifying wall near the Petit Pont[2] provides a *tempus post quem* of 1211 for *Li Fet des Romains*.

Another informative intervention provides a *tempus ante quem*. It occurs when Lucan[3] mentions Marius's several lucky escapes from death, the first of which was caused by a "German" ("Tyois") lictor who could not bring himself to obey the order to kill Marius, even though Marius was chained and helpless in a prison cell. At this point the translator intervenes to deride not only cowardly Germans but the whole "crazy" alliance of Germans, English, and Normans, the enemies of Philip Augustus:

Li Tyois entra en la chartre. Quant il ot trete l'espee et il vit Marium en la ch[a]iere, il ot tel poor, onques ne l'osa touchier. (Totes eures que il me membre de ceste chose, je tieng por fox et Anglois et Normanz, qui ont fole esperance et quident que Octes li escomeniez, que Diex et seinte Eglise ont degité, doie France envaïr par itel gent. Ne sont pas de grant hardement, quant uns d'els n'osa pas ferir de s'espee celui <qui> estoit enchaennez en une chartre et qui sa gent avoit essilliée.) (p. 365, lines 4–11)

(The German entered the prison. When he had drawn his sword and saw Marius in the chair [chains/prison?], he was so frightened that he dared not touch him. [Every time I recall this incident, I think the English and the Normans are crazy when they entertain the foolish hope and actually believe that Otto the excommunicate, rejected by God and Holy Church, will invade France with such a race. They are not very brave when one of them did not even dare to strike with his sword a chained man in prison who had been outlawed by his own people.])

The translator's mention of Otto and the Anglo-German-Norman alliance serves to date the appearance of *Li Fet des Romains* after the middle of 1213 but before July 1214, and his anger provides a fascinating glimpse of aggressive/defensive attitudes in Paris on the eve of the battle of Bouvines. Philip, soon to be called "Augustus," was steadily consolidating his authority by every possible means, and the translator obviously perceived the potential interest of Julius Caesar's past conquests in Gaul to the present inhabitants of the region.

A third intervention is equally topical. The translator comments on personal resemblances between Caesar and his king, casually introducing a comparison between the two as if their similarities had only just struck him. The precipitating context is Suetonius's description of the young Julius Caesar:

> Quant ge lis de Juilles Cesar que Luces Silla l'apeloit le valet mau ceint, si me membre de monseignor Phelipe le roi de France, que l'en pooit bien apeler le valet mau pingnié quant il estoit joenes, car il estoit torjors hericiez. (p. 18, lines 29–32)

> (When I read of Julius Caesar that Lucius Sulla used to call him "the badly girt lad," it reminds me of my lord Philip the king, whom one could certainly have called a "dishevelled varlet" when young because he was always bristlingly untidy.)

The translator could have developed the physical comparison further, judging from a description of Philip by the canon of St-Martin-des-Tours, Paien Gastinel.[4] Many of the attributes there ascribed to Philip (Catholicism apart) would apply also to Julius Caesar:

> forma venustus, corpore decens, capite calvus, facies laetus, potui ciboque deditus, luxuriae pronus,[5] amicis largus, inimicis avarus, in machinis peritissimus, fide catholicus, consilio providus, dicti tenax, judex velox et rectissimus, in victoriis fortunatissimus.

> (well built and physically handsome, bald headed, cheerful face, fond of drinking and eating, prone to *luxuria*, generous to his friends, mean to his enemies, highly expert in machinations, a good Catholic, prudent in his counsel, faithful to his word, quick and highly accurate in judgment, much favored with victories.)

However, the translator uses the sartorial reminiscing to introduce a more calculated observation:

> Ne il n'a pas mains de sens en lui que il ot en Juilles Cesar, fors seulement de letres, ne n'a pas meins eü affere que Juilles ot; et encontre ce que J<uilles> fu letrez, est li rois sanz malice, car la letreüre aguisa Juilles a meint malice. (p. 18, line 32; p. 19, line 2)

> (And he has no less intelligence than Julius Caesar, save for literacy. Nor has he had less responsibility than Julius; and against the fact that Julius was lettered, the king is without malice, for literacy often incited Julius to *malitia*.)

Highlighting the king's "sens" (intelligence) is not an empty compliment. The prologue of *Li Fet des Romains* attributes Rome's dominance to a trinity of assets, "sens, force et proece" (intelligence, force, and prowess). If Philip's "sens" is superior to Caesar's, if he shows "force" and "proece," and if, to cap it all, Catholic Philip is morally superior to pagan Julius Caesar, there is no reason to doubt that the French monarch is headed for even greater successes than Caesar in a new Gaul. As the translator pregnantly remarks when he begins his translation of the *Bellum gallicum*, "France estoit molt granz au tens Juilles Cesar" (France was very large in Julius Caesar's day, p. 79).

It should be noted that not all of Philip's contemporaries would have agreed that he lacked malice. A dissenting opinion came, not surprisingly, from the other side of the Channel, when William of Newburgh deplored the rift between the kings of France and England, and accused Philip of avid *malitia* with intent to harm and without respect for honour.[6] As for Philip's lack of literacy, it is clear that other contemporary courts, for example, Champagne, Blois, Flanders, Hainaut, and, in the south, the Angevin court, actively cultivated the arts, while the royal court in Paris appears to have had no overwhelming interest in literary pursuits and in *jeux de salon*. The most celebrated complaint about the royal family's lack of appreciation was made by Conon de Béthune, although it was his Artois dialect and lexicon rather than the quality of his verse that precipitated royal rudeness. The complaint provides a glimpse into the court's real priorities, which were more political than literary:[7]

> La Roïne n'a pas fâit ke cortoise
> Ki me reprist, ele et ses fieus, li Rois.

Encoir ne soit ma parole franchoise,
Si la puet on bien entendre en franchois;
Ne chil ne sont bien apris ne cortois.
S'il m'ont repris se j'ai dit mos d'Artois,
Car je ne fui pas norris a Pontoise.

(The Queen did not act courteously
When she made fun of me, she and her son.
My speech may not be French
But it is certainly understandable in French;
And they are not well informed or courteous
If they corrected me for using Arras speech,
For I was not born in Pontoise.)[8]

Thus, it is unlikely that Conon's mention of Marie de Champagne *qua* patroness of courtly poetry provoked the royal family to rudeness as much as the harsh political realities in which the young king was "déja terriblement et inexorablement enfoncé" (already horribly and inexorably enmeshed).[9]

More needs to be said about the translator's praise of royal illiteracy. Our enterprising anonymous compiler/translator knew the king from adolescence onwards and felt entitled to express opinions about his lack of literacy, of which he apparently approved as much as he approved of Philip's improvements to the city. Among Philip's improvements, it should be remembered, was the foundation of the University of Paris, and since the translator appears to have worked independently; has the magisterial habit – *[dé]formation professionnelle*? – of interrupting his translation with personal asides to put across new material; and is given to mediating between academic discourse and the vocabulary of "ces lais genz" (those laymen), is it possible that he worked from a university context? That is the opinion of Bernard Guenée,[10] and it would explain why the translator had access to commentaries and glosses from other schools (Orléans for one);[11] why he gave no indication that the king (or indeed anyone) has requested his monumental biography of Caesar; and why the king's improvements to Paris were, for him, the king's crowning glory. In the light of such achievements, the king's literacy was irrelevant, not to mention the fact that royal illiteracy preserved the clerical domain of learning and imparting learning. Within that domain, the revelation of his own name and situation had no relevance to him, however, and his "Ge" (I) remains anonymous throughout *Li Fet des Romains* as he builds bridges between Latin and vernacular history-writing.

Because of the novelty of his initiative, he is unusually conscientious in explaining its premises. Although he has not participated in the events he narrates, his basic assumptions about history do not differ from those of our first four historians. Truth separates history from fable; history records what is worthy of being remembered; and the eyewitness is the best guarantee of historical truth. Now, however, the words he "quotes" are from literary sources, not all of whom were eyewitnesses to the events they narrate, and their words are being translated into the French vernacular, adding one remove to the process of quotation.

In *Li Fet des Romains* an Isidorean tenet that was not relevant in the *Histories, Gesta Francorum,* or *La Conquête de Constantinople* comes into play, *viz.,* that pagan histories may be useful in certain circumstances.[12] The literary prestige of the *auctores* remained unchallenged in the Middle Ages, but their authoritativeness in a modern history was more dubious. It might demand assessment, revision, or, at the very least, explanation. Issues of authority are therefore discussed more than once. And if through lack of information the translator was not able to render unto Caesar all the things that were Caesar's (most notably the *Bellum gallicum*), he never failed to render unto God the things that are God's, touting the edifying possibilities of ancient history in his prologue.

Occasionally he speaks in his own voice through the first-person pronoun "je" (who is never identified). Sometimes quoted material is presented as if it were his own. More usually, however, sources are – with notable exceptions – identified, and if the source narrative is supplemented with material of his own invention, he conscientiously signals the fact in a process that is not so much self-referencing as self-justifying.

Contributing to the unity of the whole is his careful control of the direction of his complex narrative, making it vivid with stylistic features from the vernacular, for despite his rhetorical background and Latin learning, his style is not pretentious. An important feature that contributes to its variety is his discretionary deployment of direct speech, often converted from the indirect speech passages of his sources. For example, Suetonius reported in *Vitae* book I, para. 45, section 3 that Sulla frequently warned the senators to beware of young Julius Caesar, "the loosely girt lad" ("ut male praecinctum puerum caverent"). The translator renders Sulla's warning correctly but more vividly by turning it into the direct warning "Gaitiez vos deu valet mal ceint" (Watch out for the loosely belted boy, p. 18, line 26).

His translation of longer indirect speech passages adds vividness also by exploiting the rich freedom of medieval tense usage. A comparison of Caesar's indirect reporting of Cicero's meeting with the Nervii envoys[13] and the translator's more colourful rendering is informative. Caesar's no-frills narration was:

Facta potestate eadem quae Ambiorix cum Titurio egerat commemorant: omnem esse in armis Galliam; Germanos Rhenum transisse; Caesaris reliquorumque hiberna oppugnari. Addunt etiam de Sabini morte: Ambiorigem ostentant fidei faciendae causa. Errare eos dicunt, si quidquam ab his praesidi sperent, qui suis rebus diffidant; sese tamen hoc esse in Ciceronem populumque Romanum animo, ut nihil nisi hiberna recusent atque hanc inveterascere consuetudinem nolint: licere illis incolumibus per se ex hibernis discedere et quascumque in partes velint sine metu proficisci. Cicero ad haec unum modo respondit: non esse consuetudinem populi Romani accipere hoste armato condicionem.

(When given the chance to speak they recount the same things that Ambiorix had asserted to Titurius: that the whole of Gaul was in arms; the Germans had crossed the Rhine; that the winter quarters of Caesar and the rest were under attack. They add a mention also of Sabinus's death: they showcase Ambiorix to inspire trust. They say they are wrong to hope for any protection from those who are in desperate straits themselves; this, however, is their own frame of mind toward Cicero and the Roman people, that they refuse them nothing save winter quartering and are unwilling that this practice should become an established one: they may depart without hindrance from their winter quarters and set off without fear in whatever direction they wish. To these words Cicero replied only one thing: that it was not customary for the Roman people to accept terms from an armed enemy.)

The translator's version is no different in content – if one discounts the addition of a few clarifying specificities – but new stylistic features from the vernacular bring the narrative to life. Of particular interest is the translator's habit of mixing modes of reporting, direct speech alternating with indirect speech including free indirect speech (now often called *le style indirect libre* [free indirect style] and erroneously credited to Flaubert as a nineteenth-century invention).[14]

Quant il fu venuz avant, ce meïsme que Ambiorix ot dit a Tyturius li proposerent: que tote France s'estoit conjuree contre Romains; li Sesne avoient le Rin passé en lor aide; ja estoient ocis Tyturius et Cocta otote une legion, et firent venir avant Ambiorix en tesmoign de la chose; fox estoit Cyceron, se il cuidoit avoir secors par Cesar ne par les autres legions, qui autresi grant mestier avoient d'aide come il. "Neporquant," distrent il a Cyceron, "nos n'avons nule male volenté vers toi ne vers le pueple romain, mes ne volons pas acostumer que les legions yvernent entre nos; et, se tu voloies, tu porroies ta legion mener quel part que tu voudroies sauvement fors de ceste terre. Nos ne queronmes el." Cycero respondi: "Li pueples de Rome n'a pas en costume de reçoivre nule condicion ne nul plet de son son anemi armé." (p. 200, lines 9–22)

When he came forward, they proposed to him exactly what Ambiorix had said to Titurius: that the whole of France was sworn to arms against the Romans; the Germans had crossed the Rhine to aid them; Titurius and Cotta were already killed along with one legion, and they pointed to Ambiorix as clear evidence; Cicero was crazy, if he expected to get help from Caesar or the other legions, who had just as much need of aid as he did. "Nevertheless," they said to Cicero, "we bear no ill will toward you or toward the Roman people, but we do not want to establish the practice of having the legions winter over in our territory; and, if you wished, you could take your legion in safety wherever you wished except here. That is all we ask." Cicero replied: "The Roman people is not in the habit of accepting any condition or bargain from its armed enemy.")

(For other uses of direct speech, for example in his mimicry of Lucan, see this volume, pp. 96–8).

The following is the overall structure of our translator's ambitious compilation of multiple sources. For the introduction, two paragraphs are taken from the prologue from Sallust's *De Catilina*[15] and personalized with a paragraph of the translator's own. A chunk of Isidore of Seville's *Etymologiae* explains the unfamiliar terminology of Rome's *cursus honorum*, then Suetonius and Sallust are used in tandem for Caesar's early career in Rome. Relevant parts of Flavius Josephus's *Bellum Judaicum* and Petrus Comestor's *Historia* are borrowed for events in the east, then the translator returns briefly to Suetonius before launching into the substantial task of transferring Caesar's *Commentarii de bello gallico* into the vernacular. Almost as substantial is the material on Rome's Civil War, for which Lucan's 10 books of the *Bellum civile* are the main source. After that, he returns to Suetonius for Caesar's last days in Rome. In addition, a dozen minor sources are interspersed throughout: the Bible, St. Augustine's *De civitate Dei*, St. Jerome's *De viris illustribus*, Eusebius, the *Alexandri Magni iter ad Paradisum*, Virgil, Ovid, Geoffrey of Monmouth and/or Wace, the *Roman de Thèbes*, and the *Roman d'Alexandre*. Our discussion of the quotation practices will follow his own ordering of these disparate sources, and will, for convenience, be divided into two chapters representing his two main sources: the *Bellum gallicum* (written by an eyewitness) and the *Bellum civile* (*not* written by an eyewitness and therefore posing various problems that the translator frankly discusses for the benefit of his public).

The first two paragraphs of *Li Fet des Romains* are a lightly Christianized and modernized translation of the first two paragraphs of Sallust's *De Catilina*.[16] The translator does not acknowledge the debt, choosing to pronounce *ex cathedra* Sallust's exhortation that man should cultivate the qualities that distinguish him from other animals. He proceeds similarly with Sallust's other observations, and his first citation of a Latin author occurs when he quotes a dictum he attributes to Cicero: "Lors se estudioit chacuns plus volentiers en son enging aüser en sens que en amonceler richeces, que nus huem n'a fors a prest. Ainsi le tesmoigne Cycero, qui dist: 'Ce qui me puet estre tolu n'est pas moie chose'" (At that time every man was more intent on using his ingenuity to reasonable purpose than on accumulating wealth with it, for no man has anything except on loan. Cicero is a witness to that, saying, "What can be taken from me is not really mine," p. 2, lines 8–11).

The closest Ciceronian sentence appears to be: "quod viro forti adimi non potest, id mihi manet et permanebit" (what cannot be taken from a strong man stays with me and will remain with me, *Ad quirites post reditum* book II, section 19). This so-called quotation from Cicero may have been influenced also by the parable of the talents (Matthew 25, 14ff.), in which riches are a provisory loan. The fact that there is no such sentence in the whole Ciceronian corpus is ironic, given its message that what can be lifted is not really his! Equally ironic is the fact that in a prologue taken from Sallust, Cicero is the first and only name to be cited, yet Cicero's works seem less familiar to the translator than those of his four main authors. Ignorant of the political connotations of "novus homo,"[17] for example, he says of Cicero, "Marcus Tullius Cycerons estoit lors venuz manoir a Rome n'avoit pas lonc tens" (At that time Marcus Tullius Cicero had not long been resident in Rome, p. 25, lines 3–4). This was why, he explains, many nobles found the candidature for office of the "home novel et estrange" (new, foreign man) unacceptable (ibid., line 7).

Later, unfamiliar with the name "Cornelius Nepos," he translates Suetonius's reference to Cicero's letter to Cornelius Nepos as "A Cornille son neveu rescrist Cycero ..." (Cicero wrote to his nephew, p. 724, lines 3–4). And Suetonius's reference to the third book of Cicero's *De officiis* is suppressed although it contains significant information about Julius Caesar, *viz.*, that Euripides's words on tyranny were constantly on Caesar's lips, proving, according to many, including Cicero, that Caesar desired despotic power from his early youth. Either the minutiae of Cicero's writings did not interest the translator, *or* he calculated that they would not interest his public, *or* he knew that Cicero's Greek quotation about tyranny from someone named "Euripides" (who?) would be of little interest to them, even when translated. Fear of tyranny was a peculiarly Roman phenomenon.

For the translator, Cicero is a model of ethical behaviour, a hero – who wrote letters. After translating Sallust's account of the Catilinarian conspiracy, he concludes that Rome was delivered "par le sens Cyceron, par le conseil Caton, et par ce que Antonius et Petreius et Quintus Metellus enchacierent viguereusement Catiline, tant que il et li soen furent tot mort" (by Cicero's intelligence, by Cato's good counsel, and by the implacable pursuit of Catiline by Antonius and Petreius and Quintus Metellus until he and his cronies were all dead, p. 53, lines 29–32). The translator has so much empathy for Cicero, "li boens cle<r>s qui tant sot de plet et de rethorique (the good clerc who was so skilled in pleading and in rhetoric, p. 506, lines 11–12), that he invents some heroic exploits for him, including rousing words of his own invention to demonstrate "the good clerc's" surprisingly pungent verbal skills (see this volume, p. 101). For the invented material he draws on vernacular sources that his thirteenth-century public would appreciate, and provides them with several pages in the style of the *chanson de geste*.

The prologue's treatment of quotation, Cicero's and otherwise, is indicative. This historical compilation will be a cooperative venture in which the translator, anonymous to the end, cooperates with the greats to record the lives of other greats for a greater good. Quoting Sallust's words in the prologue as if they were his own, he lauds "those who choose reason and uprightness over carnal pleasure, and those who perform great deeds *or record them*," and gives this as the reason why "we" ("nos") shall now write "les gestes as Romains" (the deeds of the Romans, p. 2, lines 21–2).

Isidore of Seville is the next of the unnamed greats. The translator appropriates a list of the political offices in pre-imperial Rome from

Etymologiae IX, 4, but Isidore is not named specifically here or anywhere in *Li Fet des Romains*. At most he is honourably designated "L'Escriture"[18] ("Scripture," i.e., the authoritative body of recorded material that medieval *clergie* accepted as reliable) – a citation that is likely to confuse certain modern readers who might interpret it as "The Bible says."

It is some time – Chapter 8, in fact – before the translator names his first major source, Sallust. Coopted anonymously into the prologue's "we," then used in tandem with Suetonius for Caesar's early career in Rome, Sallust is eventually identified when he makes a particularly damning assessment of Catiline: "Luces Catiline, ce dist Salustes, fu de noble lignage, de grant force de cors et de grant hardement de cuer; mes de maliciex engin fu" (Lucius Catiline, according to Sallust, was of noble birth, had great physical strength and great courage, but his intent was evil, p. 21; lines 21–3). The sentence is not an actual rendering of any sentence written by Sallust, but is a fair summary of Sallust's vituperative attacks upon his anti-hero in *Catilina* V and XVI, 5. Visibly subjective, it is not a judgment about the past that the translator can personally endorse, and he pins it on Sallust. Also the mention of Sallust provides him with a specific name to prove a point he made in the prologue that "the ancients" were wont to debate the relative merits of "force de cors," "vertu," and "sens de cuer" in the promotion of "chevalerie": "Granz estrivemenz fu entre les anciens por savoir coment chevalerie poet estre plus essauciee, ou par force de cors, ou par vertu, ou par sens de cuer" (There was much debate among the ancients over whether warfare is best carried out by means of physical force, virtue, or a courageous heart, p. 1, lines 13–15). Sallust is the first of those ancients in *Li Fet des Romains* to weigh in on "force de cors" or "sens de cuer": Catiline is a prime example in *Li Fet des Romains* of physical strength and courage gone bad.

Sallust's name lends weight to another aphoristic judgment whose words are only an approximation, not a quotation, of what Sallust said. Sallust commented nastily of Catiline's third wife Aurelia that "quoius praeter formam nihil umquam bonus laudavit, quod ea nubere illi dubitabat" (with the exception of her body, no good man ever praised anything about her except the fact that she at first hesitated to marry Catiline [*De Catilina*, 15]). The translator renders this as "Molt estoit bele fame; mes, si con dist Salustes, en li n'ot onques bien qui a loer feïst, ne mes que ele refusa eu coumencement a estre espouse Catiline. Ele ne fist onques autre bien dont ele deüst avoir los" (She was a very beautiful woman; but, as Sallust said, there was never any praiseworthy good in her except that at first she refused to marry Catiline. She never did any other good thing to deserve praise, p. 22, lines 12–15). The translator accepts no responsibility for the spicy judgment, but is happy to include it – with some tweaking! His aphoristic misrendering of "bonus" (good man) as "bonum" (good thing) may have been an "honest mistake" (whatever that modern *contresens* is supposed to mean!). It may equally well have been an intentional adjustment contributing to the prologue's aim of providing "connoissance de bien fere et de mal echiver" (the knowledge to do good and avoid evil). There should not be even a hint of encouragement in his work for a good man to praise a woman's body; and as for the sexy Aurelia, the repetitive translation makes it abundantly abundantly clear that there was no "good" in her. She should have persisted in her decision not to marry Catiline!

Three other observations are attributed to Sallust as the translator wades through the complexities of the Catilinarian conspiracy. In the morbid political climate of Rome, the Catilinarian conspiracy festered "tanta vis morbi atque uti tabes," says Sallust in section 36 (so great the power of the disease like a contagion). Indeed, the disease was so pervasive that, amazingly, nobody from the whole conspiracy came forward to accuse or to reveal the matter. The translator abbreviates this dire chapter by extrapolating: "Merveilles fu, ce dist Salustes, que nus de tote la conjuroison Catiline ne vint avant por nomer ne por descovrir la chose" (It was amazing, Sallust said, that nobody from the whole Catiline conspiracy came forward with names or revealed the affair, p. 30, lines 17–19).

The conflict of personalities in Rome's party politics may sometimes have been as opaque to the translator as he knew it would be to his public. At such times, unable to verify Sallust's information, he merely cites him, as in the following complex attribution when Sallust says he personally heard ("audivi") Crassus openly affirming that Cicero had rigged all the accusations against him by instigating Tarquinius to finger him (Crassus). The translator simplifies this to "Salustes dit que il oï puis que Crassus disoit que tot ice li avoit fet Cycerons" (Sallust said that he heard afterwards that Crassus said that Cicero had done all this to him, p. 36, lines 1–2). Twelve lines later, in an equally confusing context of accusations and counter-accusations, the translator is unable to vouch for (or even disentangle?) the facts, and again resorts to citing Sallust: "Mes puis que il [Catulus et Piso] ne porent le consele a ce mener que Juilles Cesar fust nomez, si con dist Salustes, il aloient a chascun et disoient que Vulterius et li François l'avoient nomé …" (But when they could not persuade the consul to have Julius Caesar named as an accomplice, according to Sallust, they went around telling everyone that Vulterius and the French had named him, p. 36, lines 12–15).

If Julius Caesar's involvement in the Catilinarian affair was in dispute and the translator himself is not sure of the facts, "Sallust said" is a convenient "out" for him. Sallust clearly viewed Catulus's and Piso's accusations against Julius Caesar to be false. And since Sallust if not the translator was happy to swear that Caesar was falsely ("falso") implicated, even if there were doubts about Crassus's guilt, a reiterated "Sallust said" provides an affidavit from someone who was both reputable *auctor* and eyewitness. *Li Fet des Romains* is not committed to whitewashing Caesar's actions after all, but to presenting them because they can provide useful lessons.

Three other instances where the compiler mentions Sallust by name could be organizational, to mark the direction of the compilation: "Ici endroit parole Salustes des vertuz de Juilles Cesar et de Caton, et de lor valor; et conmence einsi …" (Here Sallust speaks of the virtues of Julius Caesar and Cato, and their valour; and he begins like this, p. 44, lines 11–12); "Apres revient Salustes a sa matere et dist …" (After this Sallust returns to his subject and says …, p. 45, line 27); "De ses paroles trove[n] l'en assez escriz, si come celi de Saluste[s] ou il escuse les conpaignons Catiline" (One can find many of his words on record in the writings of, for example, Sallust where he [Caesar] pardons Catiline's associates, p. 724, lines 9–10). Significantly, all three citations centre on Caesar, and all contain Sallust's presentation of Caesar's qualities and achievements. Hence the translator is able to affirm unequivocally, on Sallust's authority, that Caesar exhibited both eloquence and virtue in a murky affair.

A more substantial source for *Li Fet des Romains* than Sallust is Suetonius. Visibly inspired by the *Vitae Caesarum*, the translator states in the prologue his intention to compile biographies of Rome's 12 emperors – a project that never materialized. Although unnamed in the prologue, Suetonius is from the beginning a key member of the team, who with the translator will write this project: "Por ce escrivrons nos ci ilueques les gestes as Romains … Et comencerons nostre conte principalment a Juille Cesar, et le terminerons a Domicien, qui fu li douziemes empereres" (For this reason we shall record here the deeds of the Romans … And we shall begin our narrative first with Julius Caesar, and shall end it with Domitian, who was the twelfth emperor, p. 2, lines 21–6). Used selectively at first in the chapters about Caesar's early career, Suetonius remains unnamed until Sallust's account of the Catilinarian conspiracy is finished. When, against Caesar's pleadings, the conspirators have been condemned to death, Suetonius's name is introduced as the new source to replace Sallust (p. 53, line 33, and page 54, line 9). His name is cited also when the translator is interweaving Suetonius into Lucan's material (as on p. 352, line 26; p. 357, line 4; and p. 711, line 8).

Outside these routine identifications, the citation of the *auctor* is quirky. It underwrites details like Caesar's unruly horse (p. 726, line 29), the number of stab wounds in Scaeva's shield (p. 729, line 30), and the outstanding ability of Caesar's nephew Augustus (p. 697, line 27). The phrase "Suetonius said" also underwrites a prognostication of Caesar's approaching death, written in Greek on a tablet that was unearthed at Capua in the tomb of Capys. It warned that "quandoque ossa Capyis detecta essent, fore ut Ilio prognatus manu consangineorum necaretur magnisque mox Italiae cladibus vindicaretur" (when Capys's bones were unearthed, a descendant of Ilium would be killed by the hand of kinsmen, and would be subsequently avenged at great cost to Italy, *Vitae* I, 81).

The context of this particular citation may seem more than usually convoluted: a prophetic utterance, paraphrased from Greek into Latin by Suetonius, is guaranteed as "true" by Cornelius Balbus, who was an intimate friend of Caesar; is now validated by the translator's phrase "Suetoines dist," and then re-validated by a "truth guarantee," a device that by the thirteenth century was a favourite convention to validate purportedly authentic words, however dubious the circumstances.[19] The mention of Suetonius's name would seem to add one more link to the chain of (un)believability for a piece of fourth/fifth-hand reporting. It should be remembered, however, that in his weighing of the true against the false as he compiles Caesar's biography, the compiler remains committed to Isidore's definition of history, which opposes it to fable,[20] and Suetonius, his source, has urged his readers not to dismiss the prophecy as fable: "Cuius rei, ne quis fabulosam aut commenticiam, auctor est Cornelius Balbus, familiarissimus Caesaris" (Lest anyone suppose that this thing is a fable or a fabrication, its author is Cornelius Balbus, an intimate of Caesar's, *Vitae* I, 81). The translator therefore follows suit, and urges *his* public not to dismiss the ominous prophecy as fable: "Ne tienge nus ceste parole a fable, car Suetoines dist que Cornilles li Baubes, qui mout fu privez de lui, Cesar, le tesmoigne einsi" (Let no one consider this to be fable, for Suetonius says that Cornelius Balbus, who was an intimate of Caesar's, attests to it, p. 739, lines 5–7). What more could a medieval translator of history provide than an *auctor* who, informed by a reliable eyewitness, vouched that his facts were not fable?

The quotation on Capys's tomb has further interest in this book because it presents a problem that plagues translators even today, *viz.*, how best to translate quotations in a foreign language. Like Suetonius, who translated the original Greek into Latin, our translator usually opts to transfer a quotation into the language of his contemporary public. His handling of Caesar's (now) most famous Latin dictum "veni, vidi, vici" (I came, I saw, I conquered) is typical. The three words were originally displayed on a sign ("titulum") during Caesar's Pontic triumph (*Vitae I*, xxxvii). The translator explains (erroneously) that Caesar "spoke" the three words for all to hear, then translates Caesar's boast into French and gives Suetonius's explanation of the meaning: "et dist trois paroles en cele procession oiant toz: 'Je sui venuz, j'ai veü, j'ai veincu.' Par si bries paroles, ce dist < Suetoines >, senefia que il ot eüe cele victoire em poi de tens" (and he spoke three words in this procession for all to hear: "I came, I saw, I conquered." By such short words, Suetonius said, he signified that he had won this victory swiftly, p. 711, lines 21–4).

This word-by-word rendering makes it obvious that Caesar's snappily alliterative aphorism is as yet unknown to the French public: this is probably its first appearance on the European stage. Equally obviously, the translator is not committed to transmitting snappy Latin *bons mots*, however much he may have appreciated their snappiness or realized their potential for the future. Substance was all. Thus several things may be concluded from the translator's rendering of "veni, vidi, vici." His inclusion of Suetonius's name reminds his public that the explanation of the dictum[21] is not his own; he is not even underwriting it and may even question its correctness; it would take several centuries for "veni, vidi, vici" to become Caesar's best known dictum, quotable in Latin with no vernacular translation given and no authoritative source needed.

The decision to render classical *bons mots* into French made sense.[22] One or two quotations in Latin defy this norm and remain in their original language, for whatever reason. Both are from Isidore of Seville, and both are tweaked to fit the circumstances. One cites Virgil, who is cited in Latin for information he gives about Caesar's lineage, although the two lines are not a direct quote from the *Aeneid* – Isidore[23] is the hidden informant: "De ce dist Virgiles: 'Julius a magno demissum nomen Iulo'" (The name Julius descending from the great Iulus). Presumably because the Latin quote would be accessible only to the Latin-literate, the translator follows it with this explanation in French: "ce est a dire que Juilles descendié deu lignage Enee, qui ot un fiuz qui ot non Iulus, dont li nons de Juilles fu estraiz" (which is to say that Julius came from the lineage of Aeneas, who had a son called Iulus, which gave rise to the name Julius, p. 8, lines 7–10). The citation of Virgil's name proves nothing about the translator's knowledge or ignorance of the *Aeneid*, but it lends weight to the already weighty matter of Caesar's genealogy.

A second quotation of what "Virgil [is supposed to have] said," some of it in Latin, concerns the even weightier matter of Last Things. It reveals the complexity of the translator's quotation practices when classical and Christian authority conflict. Compressing Lucan's description of the Sibyl at Cumae, who in her Apollonian frenzy knew the end from the beginning, the translator first adds a disclaimer to "what Lucan said" about her: "Ele vit iluec le premier jor et le derenier dou monde, la mesure de la mer, le nombre de la gravele, *ce dist Lucans; qui veust, si l'en croie*" (She then saw the first day of the world and its last day, the compass of the ocean, the sum of the sand, says Lucan; believe *that*, whoever wants to, p. 454, lines 18–20; my emphasis). He then cites Virgil in "Ceste sibile et cele qui fu nee en l'isle de Cusmo,[24] dont Virgiles parole, prophetizierent princepaument de Christ et dou jor dou joïse et des Romains. Et ceste sebile qui fu de Cusmo fist vers dou joïse et de l'avenement Jhesucrist" (This Sibyl and the Sibyl born on the island of Cusmo [*sic*] about whom Virgil speaks, prophesied principally of Christ and of the Last Judgment and of the Romans. And the Sibyl from Cusmo composed verses about the Last Judgment and the Coming of Jesus Christ, p. 454, lines 23–7). Again his source is actually not Virgil but Isidore's "Ipsa est et Cumaea, de qua Vergilius ..." (This Sibyl is from Cumae, concerning whom Virgil ..., *Etymologiae* VIII, 8), which he then perverts by suppressing Isidore's quote from Virgil: "Ultima Cumaei venit iam carminis aetas" (Now came the last age of the Cumaean song, *Eclogues* IV, 4). Instead, he substitutes two familiar medieval Latin lines about the Last Judgment: "Judicii signum tellus sudore madescet;/E celo rex adveniet per secla futurus" (The earth will become moist with sweat as a sign of the Last Judgment;/And the future everlasting king will come from Heaven, p. 454, lines 28–9). This interplay of authority, with Lucan, a Sibyl, Isidore, and Virgil ultimately yielding pride of place to two familiar lines of Christian prophecy in medieval Latin, must have required careful thought and some (somewhat unsuccessful!) juggling. If the words attributed to Virgil were not the words Virgil actually wrote, and if Isidore was the hidden informant, the shift was trivial, however, in comparison with the error that would result if the Christian compiler did not master his authors. Meanwhile, Virgil's name still serves to add weight to weighty matters like genealogy and Last Things.

The most important author, substantively, for the translator is Julius Caesar himself. The eight books of the *Bellum gallicum*[25] contain the material with which he is most comfortable, and he stays with it for pages at a time without explanatory additions. *Mutatis mutandis*, his style is closest to Caesar's, yet throughout the manuscript history of *Li Fet des Romains*, the work is introduced merely as "Li Fet des Romains, compilé ensemble de Saluste et de Suetoine et de Lucan" (The Deeds of the Romans, compiled together from Sallust, from Suetonius, and from Lucan) without reference to Caesar. Not all of Julius Caesar's works were identified as such in the Middle Ages, and the translator's own comments on the subject are informative:

> Livres fist il meïsmes de ses ovraignes, des batailles de France et contre Pompee, et espystles au senat et a Cyceron, et autres escriz assez que nus ne savoit blasmer. Ja tant ne fust en ost n'en chevalerie que il ne s'estudiast en fere escriz, lues que il avoit un poi de loisir. Il fist .ij. livres que l'en apele "Analogies," el retor de France, et .ij. au siege de Monde: "Anticatons" les apeloit, et un autre poeme, < "L'Aler" > ot non, a l'aler de Rome en Espaigne. Tot son tens voloit gaster ou en chevalerie ou en cle < r > gie, sanz les hores de boivre et de mangier et de solacier od dames. Moul fist escriz ... (p. 724, lines 16–25)

> (He himself wrote books about his achievements, the wars in Gaul and against Pompey, letters to the Senate and to Cicero, and many other irreproachable writings. He was never so involved in war or in military matters as to neglect giving his attention to his writing as soon as he had some leisure. He wrote two books entitled "Analogies" when he returned from Gaul, and two entitled "Anti-Cato" at the siege of Munda, and another poem entitled "The Journey" on the way from Rome to Spain. He chose to spend all his time either in warring or writing, except the hours he devoted to drinking, eating, and womanizing. He wrote many things ...)

The vagueness of that reference to the *Bellum gallicum* is significant. The translator is aware (from Suetonius's *Vitae* I, 56) that Caesar wrote a history of his campaigns. He even mentions the fact towards the end of his work[26] without realizing that he has himself translated seven books of the said history as well as Hirtius's supplementary eighth (although book eight's prefatory letter by Hirtius is absent). But for him, as for the Middle Ages generally, the author of the *Bellum gallicum* was one "Julien" who was supposed to have authored Caesar's material because of a cryptic inscription – the notation perhaps from a *corrector* – "Julius Celsus Constantinus uc legi" (I Julius Celsus Constantinus have read this [?] [*or*] I Julius Celsus Constantinus have read up to here [?]) at the end of each book in one group of the manuscripts.[27]

This misconception had one significant consequence that reveals the importance attached to being a known *auctor* in the Middle Ages. Throughout the manuscript tradition, *Li Fet des Romains* is advertised as a compilation of only three *auctores*, and Celsus receives the silent treatment. When, atypically, a late manuscript[28] adds Celsus's name to the multiple credits at the end of the manuscript and his name finally joins the well-known trinity in the title of an isolated fifteenth-century manuscript,[29] he remains "Celsus," not "Caesar": "*Icy en ce volume sont/ les notables et auctentiques /orateurs et historiagraphes/Saluste/Julle Celse/ Lucan/Suetosne*" (*Here in this volume are the notable and authentic/orators and historians/Sallust/JuliusCelsus/Lucan/Suetonius*, fol. 1). Furthermore, although the *Bellum gallicum* is the translator's most important source quantitatively,[30] "Celsus" is treated differently throughout the translation in that "Julius" / "Juliens" / "Celsus" is cited by name only 11 times.[31] Of those 11, 2 are routine identifications ("Ici dirons selon Julian coment il [Cesar] conquist France et Bretaigne" (Here we shall tell according to Julian how Caesar conquered France and Britain, p. 75, lines 14–15); "Ici comence Juliens conment Cesar conquist France" (Here Julian begins his narration of how Caesar conquered France, p. 79, rubric). A third naming occurs when Caesar digresses into a description of the Gauls and the Germans – "quoniam ad hunc locum perventum est" (since this point in the narrative has been reached, *B.g.* VI, 11) – ensuring that there is no misunderstanding about the person responsible for digressing. Having clarified the identity of that first "nos," the translator then adds a phrase or two of his own using, this time, his compiling "we": "Et por ce, dist Julius Celsus, que nos somes a cest leu venu, nos vodromes ci endroit parler des mors et des costumes de France et de Sessoigne, et quel difference il a des uns as autres, *ce est des Sesnes as François; ne messerra pas en nostre livre*" (And since, says Julius Celsus, we have reached this point, we shall speak here about the habits and customs of France and Germany, and what difference there is between them, *that is between the French and the Germans; it will not be inappropriate in our book*, p. 219, lines 21–4; my emphasis). Caesar's digression on the habits and customs of "France" and "Germany" clearly will not come amiss in "our book" either! A fourth name-drop signals when the digressive description has come to an end: "Apres retorne Julius Celsus a sa mature et dit …" (After this Julius Celsus returns to his subject and says …, p. 229, lines 1–2).

On one occasion, the identity problem posed by the word "nos" is greater than the translator can tolerate without a more substantial intervention because, even without knowledge that the author of *The Gallic War* is Caesar, he cannot fail to perceive the author's authoritativeness. Anticipating the same question from his public – who *is* this mystery man who is able to explain Caesar's tactical, political, and psychological motivation and even penetrate Caesar's innermost thoughts? – he is impelled to fabricate a lie (modern editors might term it a "scholarly hypothesis") to validate his author's credentials. When the ever-curious Caesar tries to get some information about a midwinter night that lasts 30 days in Britain's mid-Channel islands ("de quibus insulis nonnulli scripserunt dies continuos triginta sub bruma esse noctem"; concerning which islands some people have written that in winter night there lasts 30 full days [*B.g.* V, 13]),[32] he remarks on the fruitlessness of "our" inquiries: "Nos nihil de eo percontationibus reperiebamus, nisi certis ex aqua mensuris breviores esse quam in continenti noctes videbamus" (We learned nothing about this matter when we inquired, but by precise water measurements we noted that the nights were shorter here than on the Continent, *B.g.* V, 13). To justify the right of "nos" to speak for Caesar, the translator adds two phrases explaining that eyewitness "Julian" had been Caesar's constant companion in Britain. Caesar's sentence now reads: "nos en demandames assez as païsanz de Bretaigne, *dist Juliens qui ce livre fet, car nos i fusmes avec Cesar*" (We asked the inhabitants of Britain many questions about this, said Julian, the author of this book, for we were there with Caesar, p. 184, lines 24–6; my emphasis).

The invention is understandable. Who could have guessed that the great *imperator* himself would execute his memoirs of Gaul in the misleading form of a third-person narrative? "Nos" needs clarification; a modern editor confronted with the same pronoun might reach similar conclusions, so our translator, lacking the modern device of footnotes, melds his hypothetical explanation into the narrative, validating its credentials with fabricated authority. The explanation that "Julian" was physically present with Caesar in Britain would convince a medieval public of the eyewitness experience of Celsus. For his lie the translator had the greatest authority of all: "Scripture" (i.e., Isidore of Seville). Isidore is ultimately responsible for the mendacious "car nos i fusmes" (for we were there) because of his categorical statement in *Etymologiae* I, 41, that "Apud veteres enim nemo conscribebat historiam, nisi is qui interfuisset, et ea quae conscribenda vidisset" (Among the ancients no one wrote history except the eyewitness who had been present and had seen what was to be recorded). This was sufficient reason for the translator's not unreasonable hypothesis. For good measure, the translator also upgrades Caesar's anonymous written sources here. Caesar had said "nonnulli scripserunt" (some have written), but for the benefit of his public the translator adds to the respectability of his sources by saying "aucun *ystorien* distrent en lor escriz" (some *historians* have said in their writings, p. 184, lines 22–3; my emphasis).

These minor changes intended to enhance the authority of an unknown source come with penalties. When Caesar confides that "we have no certain knowledge" whether the Aedui are telling the truth to our Roman deputies or are acting out of treachery,[33] for example, these were the personal reflections of a brilliant strategizer trying to second-guess the enemy before making a tactical decision. When, however, the translator pins Caesar's remarks on Celsus and generalizes Caesar's uncertainty to "Mes Julius Celsus dist que l'en ne set de voir se il por ce retornerent ou par tricherie" (But Julius Celsus said that it is not known whether they returned for that reason or out of treachery, p. 242, lines 14–15), the new rendering makes the observation far less significant.

Clarification of "nos" occurs again in "nostrarum turrium altitudinem, quantum has cotidianus agger expresserat, commissis suarum turrium malis adaequabant" (they matched whatever increase was added to the height of our turrets by joining new scaffolding to theirs, *B.g.* VII, 22), which the translator renders as "Ne nos ne saviennes, dist Julius Celsus, noz tors tant lever en haut come il levoient les lor et aloignoient sor lor murs" (we could not match the height of our towers to theirs as they raised and extended them on the walls, p. 252, lines 7–9). Even in a context where there would appear to be no danger of confusing the subject of "nos ne saviennes," the translator prefers to spell it out.

The phrase sometimes goes beyond mere clarification to dissociation. In Caesar's description of the training of the Druids in Britain (*B.g.* VI, 13–14), a subject that was not irrelevant to the translator's own

life, Caesar notes that Druidic priests learn by heart a great number
of verses, sometimes over 20 years, but do not commit these verses
to writing. Also they use Greek letters for their public and private accounts. He opines that they do this for two reasons: a) they do not wish
to vulgarize the rule, and b) they do not want those learning it to become less diligent or relax the memory process. Literacy and vulgariza-
tion were important subjects for our cleric, who had a monopoly on the
first but was clearly promoting the second in *Li Fet des Romains*, and
may therefore have found Caesar's hypotheses inimical. At all events,
he categorically refuses to underwrite the tendentious opinion of his
source, saying first, "this is what Julius Celsus said," and then, even
more explicitly, "this is Julius Celsus's opinion on the subject":

> Por .ij. choses la [doctrine] lessoient a escrivre, *ce dist Julius Celsus*: por ce
> que cele doctrine ne poïst estre semee ou pueple par escrit, et por ce que
> li deciple meïssent greignor cure en retenir la de cuer, car l'en met sovant
> en nonchaloir la chose ou l'en cuide recovrer par escrit; *c'en est li quidiers
> Julius Celsus*.[34] (p. 222, lines 23–8; my emphasis)

> (They refrained from writing down the doctrine for two reasons, *according
> to Julius Celsus*: so that this doctrine would not be disseminated in writing
> among the general populace, and so that its disciples would pay greater at-
> tention to memorizing it, for one often does not value what one believes is
> recoverable in written form; *that* is Julius Celsus's opinion on the subject.)

His most specious invoking of "what Julius Celsus said" occurs after
one of Caesar's disparaging comments about the Gauls. Julius Caesar
cherished his Gallic provinces, knew them well, and wrote his seven
books on the Gallic war as an apologia for his Gallic proconsulship.
Because the showcase demonstration of his – and Rome's – power to
control that fickle and unruly race would not have made for congenial
reading in Philip Augustus's France, the translator is not averse to ad-
justing Caesar's Gallic material, providing clarifications, adding praise,
attenuating blame, and generally enhancing Gallic dignity.[35] On the occasion of an ignominious flight by the Gauls after their failed attack
upon Sabinus's Roman camp, Caesar concludes, "[U]t ad bella suscipi-
enda Gallorum alacer ac promptus est animus, sic mollis ac minime re-
sistens ad calamitates perferendas mens eorum est" ([J]ust as the Gallic
temperament is ready and willing for battle, the Gallic will is weak and
minimally resistant to the enduring of calamities, *B.g.* III, 19).

The translator couches this insulting assessment in more acceptable terms with a minor word-shift of the most ingenious sort: "The French" become "The Normans": "car, si con dit Juliens, autresi come Normenz estoient prest a movoir barate et noise por petit, ensement il perdoient les cuers et les vertuz lues que il avoient une aversité d'aucun mischief" (for, as Julian said, just as the Normans were prone to instigate rebellion and trouble at the slightest pretext, they were just as apt to lose heart and courage the minute there was a reversal involving hardship, p. 148, lines 18–21). The advantages of this rendering are evident. An insulting assessment of the Gauls now serves as useful anti-Norman propaganda,[36] it is now validated by classical authority, and "Julian" (so obviously innocent of thirteenth-century antipathies!) takes the rap. "It was Julian who said it." If the name of Julius Celsus is not as weighty as Sallust, Suetonius, and Lucan, it can still serve the translator well when he wants to invoke it.

The inventiveness with which the translator attempts to authenticate Julian should not be dismissed as irresponsible but rather as a function of his respect for the author of the *Bellum gallicum*, for authority, *and* for his public. Given his and his contemporaries' ignorance concerning Julius Celsus, it was important to guarantee the respectability of such a knowledgeable eyewitness whose history he had found eminently translatable. One harmless little fabrication gave that mysteriously omniscient narrator the authority he deserved, and a nonexistent Julian was guaranteed by his own (fabricated) words and by his (presumed) eyewitness authority the right to speak for the great Julius Caesar. *Si César n'existait pas, il fallait l'inventer – et l'appeler Celsus.*

Chapter Six

In the Words of the Author

Li Fet des Romains: The Civil War

The climate of eyewitness truth was impossible to maintain when the translator embarked upon his second largest source. Lucan was *not* an eyewitness of Rome's Civil War, and his avowed purpose in writing *De bello civili* was to blast the Caesars with all the rhetorical means at his disposal. When the translation moves from the *Bellum gallicum* to the *Bellum civile*, therefore, numerous citings of the new *auctor* reflect the complexly interactive relationship that the translator has with him. Lucan's name occurs in attribution no fewer than 92 times throughout *Li Fet des Romains*, illustrating how much the personality of Lucan obtruded upon the translator's consciousness as he attempted to present Lucan's material appropriately.

It is important to view this interpretative revisionism from a medieval perspective. Mastering one's authors was the function of every Christian writer, and it demonstrated the vitality of the classics to challenge, inspire, and (often!) provoke a contemporary world. The translation of antiquity into a thirteenth-century vernacular came with important responsibilities, therefore. When respect for a historical *auctor* inspired a translator to make a particular history available to his contemporaries, the spiritual well-being of those contemporaries must to a certain degree influence the transference process, which could not anyway, by the nature of things, be word-for-word transference. Thus in the medieval relationship of author-translator-public there was a different balance of power from that obtaining in modern translation, and the compiler of *Li Fet des Romains* does not hesitate to exercise his power over the words of his sources whenever he deems it necessary.

Modern translators generally view their responsibility to the words of the source differently. Here one may usefully cite Gregory Rabassa's discussion of metaphor:

> The translator can never be sure of himself, he must never be. He must always be dissatisfied with what he has done because ideally, platonically, there is a perfect solution, but he will never find it. He can never enter into the author's being, and even if he could the difference in languages would preclude any exact reproduction. So he must continue to approach, nearer and nearer, as near as he can, but, like Tantalus, at some practical point, he must say *ne plus ultra* and sink back down as he considers his work done, if not finished (in all senses of the word).[1]

Rabassa's translative *angst* derives from a conflict between the translator's ideal of total *re*-creation and his realization that the ideal is an impossibility. For him the authority of the author is absolute, and he openly admits subservience. In the Middle Ages, on the other hand, the interaction of author, translator, and receptor was continually modulated, and it was the task of a translator with clerical responsibilities to do the fine tuning. His direct references to his sources in such phrases as "Salustes dist" (Sallust said), "Suetoines dist" (Suetonius said), and "Lucans dist" (Lucan said) ostensibly highlight his debt to his sources, but citation serves him in paradoxical ways, especially with the material taken from Lucan.

The most obvious difference between what Lucan said and what the translator *says* he said is that Lucan's words were in verse, a medium suspect in the early thirteenth century as inimical to truth, whereas the translator's are in prose. (There are only three verse occurrences in *Li Fet des Romains*. Two are brief quotations from Isidore of Seville who was quoting Virgil; the words of one of these Virgilian quotations are replaced by medieval Latin lines about The Last Judgment [see this volume, p. 84]). The other context in which verse occurs is the translator's invented supplement to Lucan's narrative, where he describes Pharsalia in a style that will convey battle excitement to his modern audience, *viz.*, the style of a *chanson de geste*; see this volume, pp. 100–2).

The change is transformative, but the translator makes it without comment, never thinking to address the issue formally and extracting from Lucan's verse epic "la matere" that was suitable for a modern history. His rendering (down) of the first 10 lines of Lucan's ninth book epitomizes the procedure. His source lyrically describes the apotheosis of Pompey, whose soul cannot be held captive in a handful of ash. It bursts forth from the pyre, leaving behind the hero's half-consumed embers, then pursues a course towards the convex regions of Jove the Thunderer through the aether among half-deified shades in that region where the shadowy air joins on to the star-bearing poles:

> At non in Pharia manes iacuere favilla,
> Nec cinis exiguus tantam compescuit umbram:
> Prosiluit busto semustaque membra relinquens
> Degeneremque rogum sequitur convexa Tonantis.
> Qua niger astriferis conectitur axibus aer
> Quodque patet terras inter lunaeque meatus,
> Semidei manes habitant, quos ignea virtus
> Innocuos vita patientes aetheris imi
> Fecit, et aeternos animam collegit in orbes:
> Non illuc auro positi nec ture sepulti
> Perveniunt. (*Bellum civile* IX, lines 1–11)

> (But the spirit of Pompey did not linger down in Egypt among
> the embers, nor did that handful of ashes prison his mighty ghost.
> Soaring up from the burning-place, it left the charred limbs and
> unworthy pyre behind, and sought the dome of the Thunderer.
> Where our dark atmosphere – the intervening space between earth
> and the moon's orbit – joins on to the starry spheres, there after
> death heroes, whose fiery quality has fitted them, after guiltless lives,
> to endure the lower limit of ether, and has brought their souls from all
> parts to the eternal spheres: to those who are coffined in gold and
> buried with incense that realm is barred.) (J.D. Duff's translation)

The imagery is majestic, the science more than dubious, the metaphysics non-Christian. The translator opts therefore to become master of his author, while allowing Lucan the authority that comes from precedence. He modifies Lucan's imagery, carefully balancing Christian orthodoxy against Stoic metaphysics. His reductive translation is: "Li os et la cendre dou cors Pompee furent mis en ce petit sepulcre covert de <a>raine et d'un pou de pierres par desus. Mes li espirist, ce dist Lucans, – qui le veust si l'en croie, – s'en ala vers la lune en air" (The bones and the ash from Pompey's corpse were placed in that small sepulchre, covered with sand and a handful of stones. But his spirit – Lucan said this, whoever wishes may believe it – departed upward towards the moon, p. 574, lines 2–5).

The caveat "qui le veust si l'en croie" dissociates the translator from the pagan content of the source and demonstrates the conflict between his allegiance to his source and his responsibity to his modern public. Those shades of heroic demigods hovering in the upper air; that immediate escape of Pompey's soul without let or hindrance from its funeral pyre to meet them; and that apotheosis of pagan heroes all spelled theological error that the translator is unwilling to perpetrate. On the other hand, Lucan was an *auctor*. Thus the translator appends to line 5 a token homage: "por itant con Lucans le dist le vos rendons" (inasmuch as Lucan said this, we render it for you).

The explanation concretizes the conflict between his respect for literary authority and his historical purpose, *viz.*, responsibility to truth. Concerning the former he uses the word "autorité" occasionally and there is no question that the literary notion it conveyed – spuriousness as opposed to authoritativeness – was clearly understood. The following example involving Julius Caesar's writings is informative (particularly in view of the medieval confusion over Julius Celsus and Julius Caesar!):

> [Cesar] mout fist escriz, et enfes et bachelers et huem, mes il ne furent pas tuit publié ne mis avant. Macres, qui s'entremetoit des bibles Augustus, en lessa plusors par son conmandement, car Augustus nes vost pas toz metre en autorité. (p. 724, lines 25–9)

> ([Caesar] as a boy, a youth, and in maturity wrote many things but not all were published or saw the light of day. Macer, who was in charge of Augustus's books, set several aside by command of Augustus who did not want to vouch for the authoritativeness of all of them.)

The word "auteur"/"acteur" occurs also, albeit imprecisely. For example, the translator supplements Lucan's account of Cato's journey through Libya with the following vague allusion:

> Dejoste cel estanc coroit une iaue plesant, Lethes fu apelee, qui sonne autretant come obliement ... A meïsmes de cele iaue et de l'estanc estoit li leus ou li renomez vergiez ot jadis esté dont Ovides et *li autre auctor* parolent. (p. 592, lines 12–19; my emphasis)

(By this pond flowed a delightful river called Lethe, which means oblivion ... Alongside this river and the pond was the place where once was that famous orchard of which Ovid *and the other authors* speak.)

But the authority conveyed by this mention of curriculum authors, while presumably of literary interest to his public, is secondary to other considerations as he compiles his history.

A useful explanation of the translator's methodology and his neutralizing of pagan mythology occurs in his rendering of Lucan's digressive description of the snakes in Libya (*B.c.* IX, lines 619–761). The translator substantially shortens Lucan's ruminations on the reason for Libya's pestilences and plagues of serpents, which are replete with tales of Medusa, Pallas, Perseus, and other mythical figures. He signals the abbreviation, giving a significant explanation of his translative criteria. The explanation is multipronged, and some of it would do a fundamentalist Christian proud:

> Plus en dist encore la fable et plus en recorde Lucans. Mes por ce que ne samble pas veritez et Lucans meïsmes nel croit pas, nos n'en volons cest livre encombrer de plus; ainz volons suivre l'ordre de la vraie estoire, et nos savons bien par tesmoign de Seinte Escriture que Damlediex cria serpenz des le conmencement dou monde, et naturels chose est que tuit serpenz demorgent plus volentiers en la chaude terre qu'en la froide. Por ce en a plus en Libe que aillors ... (p. 604, lines 10–18)

> (There is much more of this fabulous material and Lucan records more of it. But because visibly it is not the truth and Lucan himself does not believe it, we do not want to load this book with any more of it; rather we intend to follow the order of true history, and we know from the evidence of Holy Scripture that Our Lord God created serpents from the world's beginning; and it is natural for all serpents to prefer living in warm regions rather than cold. This is why there are more serpents in Libya than elsewhere ...)

This *reductio* (almost) *ad absurdum* of his source demonstrates that factors transcending literal fidelity are influential upon the translation of even an esteemed *auctor*. Isidore of Seville, who like our translator believed that pagan history was useful in certain circumstances, would have approved the rejection of fable and the invocation of scripture.[2] But our cleric also bows to the science of his day with naturalistic arguments; invokes truth and order as obvious *desideranda*; and finally bows to his *auctor* with the compliment that Lucan himself gave no credence to what he "recorded" about serpents.

To protect the religious health of his public, he intrudes again during Lucan's eulogy of Cato, "parens verus patriae" (true father of the fatherland, *B.c.* IX line 601). Lucan ranks Cato above Caesar for virtue, a judgment with which the translator concurs, but which he modifies with two corrective lines:

> Que diroie je, dist Lucans, se nul grant bien qui vraiment soient en home deivent estre de nule digne renomee, et se l'en garde nuement les vertuz qui furent en Caton, *sanz la mescheance qui au derrien li avint*, de ce que sa fortune fu si aspre que il but venim por morir ainz que il *receüst Cesar a seignor*? (p. 601, lines 28–33; my emphasis)

> (What should I say, said Lucan, if any great quality men genuinely possess deserves any renown, and if one looks unadorned at Cato's virtues, *disregarding the mischance that finally befell him* when his fate was so bitter that he drank poison rather than accept *Caesar's rule*.)

That Lucan could be made to say that a Stoic's suicide to resist tyranny mars his virtue is an ironic twist of fate. But since the translator is compiling *Li Fet des Romains* to instil a "connoissance de bien fere et de mal eschiver" (knowledge to do good and to avoid evil) in his Christian public, no suicide must be categorized as "good."

Thus the 10 books of the *Bellum civile*, now called "l'estoire de Lucan" (p. 330, line 4), are sifted for their substantive content, and no attempt is made to reproduce or imitate the form in which they are couched. There is one notable exception. Lucan's emotionalism is mimicked through a rhetorical feature that can be deployed equally in Latin and the vernacular: the device of apostrophe. Apostrophe, often accompanied by the phrase "Lucans dist" (Lucan said), is a stylistic hallmark of the *Bellum civile* section of *Li Fet des Romains*, providing an economical means to tag quirky emotional exclamations from Lucan as just that, *viz.*, quirky emotional exclamations from Lucan. "Have you no shame, Caesar, that you alone enjoy your wars?" ("Non pudet, heu! Caesar, soli tibi bella placere?" *B.c.* V, 310) is rendered as "O, Cesar, ce dist Lucans, es tu si desvez que batailles plesent a toi seul? Ne vois tu que ta gent les dampne?" (p. 458, lines 24–5). (It is worth noting in passing that Lucan indicts Caesar's lack of shame – "Non pudet, heu" – whereas the translator conveys rather the "craziness" of Caesar's plan to undertake wars without the support of the armies who will fight them, yet another example of a modernized political perspective.)

Not all apostrophes are retained, of course, for in the same section the translator paraphrases Lucan's apostrophe to the gods ("Sic eat, o superi: quando pietasque fidesque/Destituunt ... /Finem civili faciat discordia bello" (So be it, o gods: When piety and fidelity are lacking ... let discord put a stop to civil war, B.c. V, lines 297–9), making it less tortuous and more appropriate: "Pres ala, ce dist Lucans, que lor descorde ne mist la guerre de Cesar a fin, ce que foi et pitiez ne porent fere" (Their discord, said Lucan, nearly ended Caesar's war, when faith and piety could not, p. 458, lines 10–12). Again, a blander version of what Lucan actually said. Similarly, Lucan's ranting at Caesar for his "unlawful wedlock" in Egypt and his "illicit offspring" is transformed into factual statement when "Pro pudor! oblitus Magni tibi, Iulia, fratres/Obscaena de matre dedit" (Shame! Forgetting Pompey, he gave Julia brothers by an obscene mother, B.c. X, lines 77–8) is explicated as "Bien avoit oblié Pompee et Julia, sa fille ... Molt l'en blasme Lucans" (He had obviously forgotten Pompey and Julia, his daughter ... Lucan reproaches him greatly for that, p. 624, lines 3–8).

The translator may alter the verb of "Lucans dist" (Lucan said) to register a shift or heightened charge in Lucan's emotional intensity. When young Cordus fearfully attempts to give proper burial to Pompey's decapitated body, Lucan, in anti-Caesarean rage, applauds Cordus's piety, exclaiming, "Quam metuis, demens, isto pro crimine poenam ...?" (What retribution for your crime do you fear, you fool?, B.c. VIII, line 781). In the translation of this, Lucan no longer "speaks" but "cries," expressing his rage in suitably modernized idiom: "Lucans li escrie en son livre: 'Diva! fols, que doutes tu? Quides tu avoir pene por le bien que tu as fet?'" (Lucan in his book cries to him: "Shame! What do you fear, you fool? Do you expect to be punished for the good thing you did?," p. 570, lines 5–6). And Lucan "reviles" ("lesdoie") the incestuous Ptolemy in: "Ici lesdoie Lucans Ptolomé et dist: 'Mauves rois forsligniez, li derrienz de cels qui de la gent Alissandre regnerent en Egypte'" (Here Lucan hurls abuse at Ptolemy, saying: "Wretched, degenerate king, last of the line of Alexander to rule in Egypt," p. 566, line 34–p. 567, line 3) in a modernized rendering of "Ultima Lageae stirpis perituraque proles/Degener ..." (Degenerate, last offspring of the doomed Lagus line ..., B.c. VIII, lines 692–3).

In this play with apostrophe, the translator rings all possible changes. Exclamations are retained as exclamations, frequently introduced by "O" or "Ha": "O, dist Lucans, Egypte!" ("Oh Egypt!," said Lucan, p. 572, line 12); "dist Lucans, O tu Rome!" ("Oh Rome!," said Lucan, p. 522, line 2). They are paraphrased as direct or indirect speech, accompanied by a vestigial "Lucans (ce) dist": "'O Thessaille! Thessaille!' dist Lucans" ("Oh Thessaly! Thessaly!" said Lucan, p. 521, lines 9–10). Or, inserting new drama of his own, the translator may convert a direct statement into an apostrophe (still adding the phrase "[ce] dist Lucans"). The attribution shifts responsibility for Lucan's impassioned anti-Caesar venting over what he calls "your crimes, Caesar" (*B.c.* VII, line 551)[3] away from the translator. Through apostrophe, the translator is able both to signal an emotionally charged assertion and to ensure an appropriate reaction if the original sense is obscured by florid presentation.

Two major sources – the glossators and the translator in the role of author – contribute silently to the laudable venture of presenting Lucan's *matere* for the instruction and entertainment of a new public. The contributions of the glossators are not easily quantifiable, and some may never now be identified. The translator incorporates their information without acknowledgment into what he calls "l'estoire de Lucain" (Lucan's history) to explain geographical, historical, mythical, and other similarly technical aspects of the source. "Lucan calls [the Rubicon] red because the earth and sand of its channel are vermilion" (p. 347, line 25–p. 348, line 1). "Lucan said that Nero in his reign blocked the seat of the Delphic oracle and forbade further access, not wishing the Romans to plot against him" (p. 452, line 33–p. 453, line 2). "Caesar built a war-weapon that Lucan calls 'vinea' because this contraption is closed at the top like a trellis, covered above with string hides to protect against pitch and boiling water, and reinforced with soil on top of that to cushion the impact of stones and spears" (p. 376, lines 4–8). None of this information derives from Lucan but from glosses, some of which have been identified.[4]

The degree to which the translator has mentally incorporated these unnamed suppliers of information into the source-material is illustrated in his treatment of the "vinea" described above. This siege-weapon figures several times in the *Bellum gallicum*,[5] to the dismay of the Aduatuci, among others. That sturdy tribe was dismayed that their walls could be threatened by the ingenuity/engineering of the puny Romans simply by making a tower roll towards them "par le sens et par l'engin des Romains" (by the intelligence and by the ingenuity/engineering of the Romans, p. 132, lines 33–4) – one of our translator's magisterial witticisms! A detailed description of the ingenious "vigne" is not provided immediately, but the translator promises "bien dirons en l'estoire de Lucan quel angin ce sont" (we shall tell you in Lucan's history what sort of engines they are, p. 330, lines 4–5). What better homage to Lucan's anonymous glossators than to make them jointly responsible for "Lucan's history"!

Some of his attributions might have been better left anonymous, adding little real authority except perhaps with a popular audience. Examples of such citations are: "aucun ystorien" (some historians, p. 184, line 22); "Erastotenes et autre greu filosofe" (Erastothenes and other Greek philosophers, p. 227, line 12); "L'en trove ... en aucune escriture" (One finds ... in some scripture, p. 349, line 30); "tex i a qui dient" (there are some who say, p. 356, line 17); "Li autre[s] dient" (Others say, p. 368, line 17); "selonc les fables ... mes selonc la verité" (according to fables ... but according to the truth, p. 397, lines 2–3); "Li un dient" (Some say, p. 454, line 21); "es autres tretiez ... et aillors" (in the other treatises ... and elsewhere, p. 522, lines 13–14); "L'en puet bien prover par escriture ... car l'en troeve lisant" (One can prove through scripture ... for one finds when reading, p. 571, lines 19–20); "si con l'estoire conte" (as history/the story says, p. 578, line 23); "la vraie estoire" (the true history/story, p. 604, line 13); "cuident aucum" (some think, p. 629, line 8); "li autre hystoristre" (the other history-writers, p. 649, line 8); "Hellespont le claime l'escriture" (Scripture calls it the Hellespont, p. 652, line 30); "le braz seint George le soelent nomer li auquant" (some call it St. George's arm, p. 652, line 31); "Auquanz i a qui cuident" (There are some who think, p. 684, line 8); "L'en tesmoigne" (It is reported, p. 719, line 4); "cuident aucun ... li autre dient" (some think ... others say, p. 721, lines 9–10); "li un dien<t> ... li autre afferment" (some say ... others affirm, p. 726, lines 23–4); "Tex i a qui dient ... Li autre dient" (There are some who say ... Others say, p. 735, line 21 and line 23); "Li un dient ... l'en troeve xxiij. en aucun leu" (Some say ... one finds 24 in one place, p. 271, lines 2–4); "Se l'en troeve en aucun leu ... ce n'est pas descorde" (If one finds in one place ... it is not a contradiction, p. 744, lines 11–12). These vague citations may have lent a certain authority in their day without substantially changing the legitimacy of the material.

Through them he forges a template for the future as he defines the function of quotation in his history-writing. As for the inventions by which our anonymous translator supplements his sources, they are readily identifiable because he himself signals them. When Lucan provides only 40 lines on the Alexandrian War, the translator complains of the inadequate coverage, saying that Lucan and Suetonius skim the subject so cursorily that no one can get a clear picture of events. He claims to have consulted three additional (impossible!) sources – Herodotus, Berosus, and Oppius – all of whom fall short also. Then, since the lacuna threatens narrative continuity, he supplies an interpolation of his own, justifying it as his way to handle in his own words what his sources did *not* say. For example, he embroiders the few facts he can glean into a fabricated interpolation narrating the deaths of Photinus, Achillas, and Pompey, and the rescue of Arsenoe from prison (the latter episode showing obvious affinities with the *roman*).[6] Blaming the inadequacy of his source, he justifies his invention on grounds of truth and clarity: "Ceste chose que nos avons ici contee de la mort Ptolomé et de Photin et d'Achillas et de la delivrance Arsenoé de la prison touche Lucans si tres briefment et si obscurement, que nus ne puet estre certefiez de la verité ne de l'ordre de l'estoire par chose que il en die" (What we have narrated here about the death of Ptolomy, Photinus, and Achillas, and about the rescue of Arsinoe from prison, is so cursorily and so obscurely treated by Lucan that no one can be certain of the truth or order of his history/story from anything he says about it, p. 651, lines 25–9).

Another interpolated episode at Pharsalia appeals to contemporary tastes by borrowing phrases and techniques from the *chanson de geste*. First the translator signals a lacuna in Lucan to legitimize himself as source, and then he fills the lacuna with his own words. He excuses the invention on the grounds that it is unthinkable, given the caliber of Pompey's followers, that they would allow themselves to be defeated in the Civil War without many great struggles and many great losses on either side (p. 522, lines 14–17). His public is encouraged through epic formulae of direct address – "la veïssiez grant dolor" (there you would have seen great distress) – to imagine the scene for themselves. The frequency of present tenses in his vivid reconstruction of the battle increases significantly, and his own fragments of epic verse betray his source of inspiration as the *chanson de geste*.[7]

As in the medieval epic, outside sources are adduced for the invented material, and although the jousting is acknowledged to be a departure from Lucan, the translator mimics epic citation of "li livres" (the book) by claiming that "we" found some of the material in an outside source, for example, "other treatises," "a book Caesar wrote about his achievements," as well as "Suetonius and elsewhere":

En la premiere assanblee que Cesar et sa mesniee firent a Pompee et au senat et as rois qui furent en la greignor legion, il i ot meinte bele joste et meint beau cop feru, dont Lucans ne parole pas; mes nos les <es>criverons cinsi con nos les avons trovez es autres tretiez, en un livre meïsmes que Cesar fist de ses fez, et en Suetoine et aillors. (p. 522, lines 9–14)

(In the first engagement between Caesar and his retainers with Pompey, the senate, and the kings who were in the larger legion, there were many fine jousts and many fine blows exchanged that Lucan does not mention; but we shall write them down as we found them in the other treatises, in a book even that Caesar wrote about his deeds, in Suetonius, and elsewhere.)

The citation is spurious and the text shows no knowledge of sources beyond Lucan. The authoritative names quoted would, however, impress the translator's public as effectively as "li livres" that epic writers cited in earlier generations.

The translator's battle episodes diverge, of course, from anything Caesar could have written in "a book about his deeds." Cicero,[8] called variously "Cyerons" and "Tuilles," splices Gabilion's head with swash-buckling prowess so that "neither helm nor coiffe was worth a glove to stop Gabilion from being cleft to the eyebrows." From that blow Tully went on to strike "Garal the Provençal,"[9] who was shrieking insults about Pompey and the Senators. Cicero avenged Pompey's cause with a blow that sliced through Garal's nose, moustaches, lips, and chin so as to bare all his teeth. Then Cicero mocked his enemy's "circumcised lips" with this powerful battle taunt: "Tenez, dist Cycerons, cil qui ceste colee vos done vos aprant que vos devez avoir les levres si circoncises, que vos ne dïez folie de cels qui doivent estre seignor" (So, said Cicero, this stroke from me will teach you that you deserve your circumcised lips to stop you saying insults about your rightful lords, p. 526, line 32–p. 527, line 2).

Horses also fight in epic combat at Pharsalia. Caesar's and Pompey's chargers hurl themselves at each other in mortal battle while their owners fight beside them. Eventually Pompey's horse falls dead, Caesar's falls paralysed, and Caesar chants over it an epic *planctus*: "Ahi! boens <destriers>! tant mar i fustes! de tant estor m'avez gité! Ja mes ne sera vostre perte par moi recovree. Ge ne prise pas de vos les tresors de .xl. citez" (Ah, my fine horse! What a fate! You rescued me from so many battles! I shall never get over losing you. The treasures of 40 cities mean nothing in comparison, p. 528, lines 20–2). Caesar is somewhat comforted, however, by the fact that Pompey's horse dies outright while *his* has still a breath of life remaining. This gives him hope of victory at Pharsalia.

Episodes like this are visibly epic in inspiration, and the translator says as much in a specific reference to *La Chanson de Roland* during his three-page development upon three lines from Lucan. At the battle of Brundisium the combatants "surpassed the exploits of Roland and Oliver." "Cil se combatoient, por neent i parlast l'on de Rollant ne d'Olivier, et ocioient de la gent Cesar a grant tas" (These men were in combat, useless even to mention Roland and Oliver, and were killing Caesar's men in great heaps, p. 383, lines 19–21). The hyperbole is epic, and the translator may be forgiven his self-congratulation when his heroes surpass even Roland and Oliver. After all, none of his interpolations, whether they treat love or war, contains an event so important as to contravene history as presented by his sources; none even moves the action forward; and all add narrative excitement by their development of epic topoi. The process is one of expansion, not progression, as the translator enhances *la matere* by *amplificatio*. The interpolated episodes in his own words are his personal contribution as he celebrates "those who perform great deeds and those who record them."

Given the pride and satisfaction that the translator/compiler/author found in composing *The Deeds of the Romans*, it is surprising that he persisted in his anonymity to the end. The reason may lie in the university context in which he worked. In a recent study of the changed climate in thirteenth-century universities,[10] Ian Wei comments, "It is possible to read about twelfth-century scholars in their own words; the way they taught, their personalities, their ambitions, their disappointments; in short, their lives, or representations of their lives. Moving towards the end of the twelfth century and into the thirteenth, however, there is very little comparable material, perhaps even none. In the thirteenth century, scholars wrote a great deal about being a scholar, but they preferred always to stress their collective identity, so that narrative accounts of particular scholarly lives did not find a place within the emerging universities." Wei attributes this to changes in the university itself, where the interests of "the masters and scholars of Paris" were now best served by a language of collectivity.

Be that as it may, the translator's prologue asserts that whether (like Sallust, Suetonius, and Lucan) those who record the great deeds are celebrated by name or whether (like Isidore of Seville, the glossators, and the translator himself) they remain anonymous, they are collectively as meritorious as the heroes whose deeds they record.

> *Cil qui plus sivent raison et droiture que delit charnel, qui font les proesces ou qui les recordent, cil font a loer.*

> (*Those who pursue reason and righteousness rather than carnal pleasure, those who perform heroic deeds or record them, they are praiseworthy.*)

Conclusion

Early medieval history-writing presents unusual challenges to the twenty-first century. Its basic assumptions appear to coincide with modern assumptions, only to confound modern expectations at unexpected moments. Its original models were to be found in Latin and Biblical histories, but these are inadequate to explain later developments. Its generic hybridity and its blend of vernacular traditions and an older heritage make it resistant to modern classifications. Much needs to be done to bridge the gap between Latin and vernacular history-writing.

It is important to avoid anachronistic treatment of an age when *historia* denoted both history and story. Insistence upon a demarcation between "fact" and "factitious" in a medieval work or upon its "degree of historicity" is counterproductive. Working backwards from the present imposes anachronistically subjective judgments that undermine the veracity of its narrative voice. An examination of medieval practices of quotation has proved to be a productive approach because it offers a window upon the literary and historical assumptions of a work, revealing both the commonalites and the originalities.

The works examined in this book were selected for their primacy. Each is in some way the first of its kind and therefore at a nexus between the old and the new. Nithard's *Historiae de dissensionibus filiorum Ludovici Pii* contains the first piece of vernacular French; the *Gesta Francorum* is the first eyewitness account of the First Crusade; *La Conquête de Constantinople* by Geoffroi de Villehardouin and *La Conquête de Constantinople* by Robert de Clari are the first chronicles in the French vernacular; *Li Fet des Romains* is the first work of ancient historiography and the first biography to appear in French. Implicitly and/or explicitly, all these works shared certain assumptions about history while differing

markedly in their ways of recording it. Their quotation practices highlight the conventions they shared and their individual reactions to
those conventions.

One basic assumption that is common to all of them is the Isidorean
tenet that history records what is worthy of being remembered; unlike
fable, it is the vehicle of truth, and that truth is best guaranteed by the
eyewitness. As Isidore formulated it, "quae enim videntur, sine mendacio proferuntur" (for things witnessed are proffered without falsehood). But if truth was in the seeing, was it also in the telling? There is
intrinsic ambiguity in the notion of medieval *historia*.

Nithard's *Historiae* were ostensibly commissioned in the cause of
truth. The author's young cousin, patron, and overlord Charles the
Bald wanted the truth of events in his reign and of Lothar's "persecution" of him and his brother Louis to be recorded for posterity. Nithard
was ideally qualified to fulfil the task, being a highly educated aristo-
crat belonging to the royal family and with access to the royal chancery.
He may even have prepared the original translated document of the
Strasbourg Oaths himself. But he states at the beginning of the third
book that the task has become disagreeable and he continues it only to
prevent ill-informed, alternative (i.e., non-truthful) versions of events
from surfacing.

His use of direct speech is sparse and iconic, serving only to highlight the most important issues. Early in the work he sacramentalizes
Lothar's public apology to his father and his public acceptance of his
father's terms for the division of the empire by casting him as the Prodigal Son, quoting Luke 15:18. His next dramatic use of direct speech is
his famous quotation of the *ipsissima verba* of the Strasbourg Oaths. If
seen in the context of his time, this was an iconoclastic move, the significance of which is usually blurred by anachronistic interpretations/
appreciations of it. If one examines the oaths in their own context, it
becomes clear that for Nithard (whose ideal imperial model was Charlemagne) the barbaric vernacular inserts were graphic representations
of the disintegration of empire into a Tower of Babel. A final quotation
makes this clear at the end of the work when he borrows the scriptural
authority of the *Book of Wisdom* to mourn the two good men in his family, then forecasts never-ending dissension for the rest: *Et pugnabit orbis
terrarum contra insensatos* (And the earth will war against the foolish).
Thus although his *Historiae* appear in many ways to fulfil the expectations of the modern historian, most especially by their inclusion of
actual documents, the context in which the oaths are embedded reveals

that this is an audacious use of quotation by a disgruntled royal historian. Judging by Nithard's personal observations, one may even wonder whether he regarded his instruction to write a history of the family's dissension as a worthy project. Perhaps he doubted whether it fulfilled history's function of recording events that were worthy of memory. Not surprisingly, his now most celebrated use of barbaric quotation was not a trendsetter. *Ipsissima verba* would not be the norm for centuries to come, and their real function in a ninth-century history that was nostalgic for the greatest emperor of them all deserves reappraisal.

The *Gesta Francorum et aliorum Hierosolimitanorum* was authored by a very different history-writer. Anonymous came from Italy, a descendant probably of a Norman immigrant family and, it would appear, a *miles literatus* (a Latin-literate soldier). His eyewitness narrative of the First Crusade, some of it written *in medias res*, appeared anonymously soon after the last major episode of the Crusade, the battle of Ascalon. The *Gesta* has no explanatory prologue and its author is unknown and uncelebrated. His only literary quotation is Biblical, but it is of the simplest sort, reflecting the sort of scriptural knowledge that would be possessed by a committed Crusader. He is obviously awed by the magnitude of the event in which he is participating; he makes no attempt to enhance it through classical authority, and his style has more affinities with vernacular epic than with, say, the *Aeneid*.

He is, however, aware of the authority accruing to him because of his eyewitness experience and at one point even flaunts it, claiming that although unable to narrate everything they did before Antioch was captured, there was no one else there, whether cleric or layman, who could record or narrate what he had seen anyway. He uses direct speech frequently, and it is this narrative feature that has given rise to the most anachronistic conjectures about his composition, even from his editor Louis Bréhier. Having decided that Anonymous is generally a terse and factual narrator, a reliable historian *avant la lettre*, Bréhier judged any direct speech passages that were *not* terse and factual to be spurious. Bréhier's touchstone of authenticity was the probability, or at least the possibility, that all speeches in the *Gesta* represented *ipsissima verba*. If not, they were "hors-d'oeuvres" that, he further hypothesized, a *second* Anonymous must have added to the original record. This was *inventio* as imaginative as the so-called "hors-d'oeuvres" of the medieval chronicler whom Bréhier insisted on creating in his own image. When Anonymous employed direct speech he was not using *ipsissima verba* (except for the Crusading battle cry and for three oddly isolated words in Greek whose function was almost certainly parodic). Direct speech was the vehicle, for example, of Pope Urban's sermon at the Council of Clermont – during which Anonymous was not present – and for the poor martyred Crusaders who died of starvation during the siege of Nicaea and cried out from heaven (during which Anonymous was present only imaginatively). Yet all these passages have a veracity of their own and are an integral part of the author's narrative voice, whether (to employ a modern metaphor) he chose to lip-sync quotations or to ventriloquize in direct speech.

Villehardouin's *La Conquête de Constantinople* is guaranteed as true by its author by virtue of his eyewitness experiences "si com cil qui a toz les conseilz fu" (as someone who was present at all the councils). His authority comes from his knowledge of the ambassadorial, negotiating, and military transactions in the Crusade, which he narrates clearly and simply. His literary quotations match this military sobriety, comprising practical proverbs, occasional Biblical references, and frequent echoes of the *chansons de geste*. His self-referencing reveals underlying complexities, however. When he quotes himself, he speaks with several voices, and the material associated with each is different. Ironically, his professional experience has made him suspect both for the material he reports (directly or indirectly) and for what he *fails* to report. The curious distribution of direct speech passages – in the first hundred paragraphs, direct speech (often in councils and contexts of negotiation or persuasion) occurs in thirty-four, in the second hundred it occurs in sixteen, in the third hundred in six, and in the fourth hundred in three – has also elicited comment. Among the various suggestions that have been made to explain the author's disproportionate use of direct speech in the first half and the supremacy of indirect narration in the second half is an evolutionary change that reflects "la démarche d'un vrai historien" (the development of a true historian). Remembering that, like the anonymous author of the *Gesta*, Villehardouin regarded Crusading as an epic enterprise, the reduction in his dramatic presentation of events through direct speech more probably reflects his personal reaction to the disheartening changes of direction in the events themselves. As the dramatic moments diminish, Villehardouin's epic vision diminishes with them. Sadly, *his* story was not destined to become history.

Villehardouin's professional role in the Fourth Crusade raises questions that are not asked of his less knowledgeable contemporary, Robert de Clari, whose *La Conquête de Constantinople* is often praised for its "veracity." Villehardoun's quotation practices reveal a highly sophisticated and multivoiced historian of epic inspiration; Robert's quotation practices have the vividness of a *conte* or *fabliau* and presume an audience that delighted in those genres. They provide more than dramatic verve, however, revealing information that would otherwise have been lost. For example, Robert's treatment of the pope's excommunication of the Venetians proves it was a known fact among rank and file Crusaders; Villehardouin is less than forthcoming on the subject. Without Robert's doge, no glimpse of Venetian attitudes to the Venetian excommunication would be available, and it is noteworthy that with the exception of Dandolo's direct speech passages, no glimpse of Venetian attitudes to their excommunication is to be found in any contemporary narration. The earliest surviving Venetian chronicles of the Crusade, compiled well after the event, were for a number of reasons unsatisfactory, the implications of their narrative being that the Venetian and other Italian Crusaders believed the pope himself had directed the Crusade to Constantinople and that the information known by a rank-and-file Frankish Crusader was withheld from the Venetians by their leaders. Here, as in many contexts, Robert's delight in detail supplements Villehardouin's prudent silences. While caution is required – *le povre chevalier* is often in error – there is a wealth of unexpected information in Robert's fascinating travelogue-cum-Crusading chronicle, and while all three of our Crusading chroniclers use the "inexpressibility topos," it is Robert who attempts the impossible with his flurries of "inexpressibles."

Li Fet des Romains adds another dimension because, sharing the historical assumptions of our first three works, it makes its practices explicit. Differing from the previous works by length, by its ambitious plan to compile and translate all known sources on Julius Caesar's life and deeds, and, of course, by the type of its quotation practices – quotation at one remove – it forges new paths in vernacular history-writing. Its compiler-cum-translator-cum-author selects from his clerical training those rhetorical processes and methods that are transferable to the vernacular, and thoughtfully explains them to his public as he goes. Familiar with academic discourse, he provides a running commentary on his sources – their reliability, their disagreements, their lacunae, and his own supplementation of them.

The self-awareness with which the translator/compiler of *Li Fet des Romains* interacts with his sources is an invaluable aid to our understanding of early medieval history-writing: the frequency with which he cites them is as informative as the contexts where he speaks in his own voice, supplements, or even presents quoted material as if it were his own. For despite differing circumstances, all our history-writers share the same definition of history that Isidore had provided centuries earlier, *viz.*, that unlike fable, history is the medium of truth. If their pursuit of that truth sometimes now confounds historical expectation, anachronistic judgments can be prevented and their essential veracity be uncovered through a proper understanding of their practices of quotation.

Afterword

Since each of the works treated in this book is in some sense the first of its kind, it is appropriate in this afterword at least to mention their afterlife. If one discounts a late, incomplete copy from the fifteenth century, Nithard's *Histories* survived in only one Latin manuscript, number 9768 in the Bibliothèque Nationale, Paris.[1] This unique manuscript, containing also Flodoard's *Annales*, dates from the end of the ninth century. It belonged originally to the monastery of St-Médard, and it is not now known whether it was copied there or elsewhere. Perhaps it was copied at St Riquier from Nithard's original. Virtually neglected for several centuries – it was mentioned only once by the anonymous thirteenth-century author of *Historia regum Francorum* – it was eventually printed in the late sixteenth century and reprinted several times thereafter. Its early obscurity is unsurprising, given Nithard's ambivalent attitude to his royal cousins and his thundering pessimism at the conclusion of the *Histories*, where he virtually invokes a plague on all their houses. The *Histories* was bound for a time to lose friends and influence nobody. Today, however, interest in the work has increased exponentially, for although it is the oldest of our texts, it is now in many ways the most modern. Its direct style is unpretentiously simple. It provides invaluable information (in spite of Nithard's personal bias) about the conflicts and negotiations during the fragmentation of Louis the Pious's empire. And Nithard's unprecedented quotation of the Strasbourg Oaths at a time when an accurate orthography for them had not been formulated has proved to be an unexpected delight (and conundrum) to modern linguists. Our examination of the literary context in which he embedded them, however, demonstrates that Nithard's own reaction to the oaths was different from posterity's.

The original manuscript of the *Gesta Francorum* is lost also, and the work survives in only three copies. It became, nevertheless, the preferred source for later historians who, while ostensibly despising its rusticity, plagiarized it shamelessly (even incorporating direct speech episodes that its twentieth-century editor Bréhier judged non-veracious). Significantly, even those medieval historians who *were* present at the Council of Clermont provided no better record than the *Gesta*'s of the pope's sermon. *Ipsissima verba*, even when papal, were clearly not expected from the ecclesiastical eyewitnesses.

Villehardouin's *La Conquête de Constantinople* survives in at least six manuscripts, demonstrating that after its composition it was relatively available in Europe. Its surprisingly abrupt conclusion was remedied by various later continuators who included events that occurred after 1207. Robert de Clari's *La Conquête de Constantinople*, on the other hand, remained virtually undiscovered for centuries in its repository in a monastery library at Corbie. It is now to be found in the Royal Library in Copenhagen, the final work in MS 487, whose other contents include the *Chronique du Ménestrel de Reims*, Jean de Flixécourt's *Roman de Troie*, the *Chronique de Turpin*, and Pierre Alphonse's *Livre du Castiement et des Proverbes*. Those titles provide the only clue – and it is a tenous one – to Robert's intended audience. More recently, however, Robert's star has been in the ascendancy, perhaps because his simple, frank, and sometimes gullible account of the Fourth Crusade has modern appeal to our politician weary century. He serves as a corrective to Villehardouin's more sophisticated narrative but is rarely in disagreement with Villehardouin on basic issues, however different his slant. Together these two participants in the Fourth Crusade present an invaluable eyewitness record of Crusading from a Frankish perspective.

It was not until 1267 that a complete description of the Fourth Crusade appeared in a *Venetian* chronicle – in the first part of Martin Da Canal's *Les estoires de Venise* – and, as Thomas Madden neatly says, it "conforms closely with what a Venetian Crusader might infer given the evidence of his eyes but incomplete information about the dynamics driving events."[2] By the fourteenth century Venetian chroniclers were drawing upon a much wider range of foreign narratives of the Fourth Crusade than their predecessors, and a version that conformed more closely to our two French narratives appeared there in the mid-fourteenth century. A complete manuscript of Villehardouin's *La Conquête de Constantinople* arrived officially in Venice in 1541, but was probably available there even earlier.

Li Fet des Romains enjoyed success in many quarters for at least two centuries and is known to have been owned by various celebrities. We may never know whether the "illiterate" Philip Augustus ever "read" it, but Charles le Téméraire enjoyed listening to stories of Rome, especially *Li Fet des Romains*. A copy of it was made in Brussels for Edward IV. Many compilers plagiarized it (among them Brunetto Latini) with or without acknowledgment. It went to Italy and Portugal, where it met with similar success. It was even printed twice by Antoine Vérard in 1490 and 1500. Its most interesting legacy is perhaps the degree to which its quotation practices persisted when translators outside France introduced it to their new audiences, replacing the Gallicisms with more appropriate references, yet still citing what the *auctores* said. Many of these later translator/compilers followed our translator by remaining anonymous. Uninterested in establishing proper credit for themselves, it was the credibility of the product that was paramount. Yet the more they cited it, the more likely they were to render it in *their* own words.

Notes

Foreword

1 The editors, Simon Gaunt and Sarah Kay, explain, "We could not include everything, and to our regret there is no discussion of medieval historiography, and much less than we would have liked of some other major works like the *Roman de Renart*" (p. 4).

2 Nithard, *Histoire des fils de Louis le Pieux* (Paris, 1926). All references will be to this edition.

3 *Histoire anonyme de la première croisade* (Paris, 1964). References are to this edition, but extensive use has been made also of the excellent edition by R.M.T. Hill, *Gesta Francorum et aliorum Hierosolimitanorum. The Deeds of the Franks and the Other Pilgrims to Jerusalem* (London, 1962).

4 Baudri de Bourgeuil/Baudri de Deuil, *Historia Jerosolimitana. Recueil des Historiens des Croisades Occidentaux (1841–1906)*, IV, p. 9.

5 There are six extant manuscripts and several modern editions. Natalis de Wailly's *La Conquête de Constantinople par Geoffroi de Ville-Hardouin avec la continuation de Henri de Valenciennes* with modern translation (Paris, 1872, 1874, and 1882) used as its base manuscript MS A (Paris, Bibliothèque nationale de France, fonds français 4972). Edmond Faral's *La Conquête de Constantinople* (Paris, 1939 and 1961) used MS O (Oxford, Bodleian Library, Laud. Misc. 587). More recently, CRAL (Centre de recherches et d'applications linguistiques) produced *Josfroy de Vileharduyn, La Conqueste de Costantinople* (Nancy, 1978) used MS. B (Paris, Bibliothèque nationale de France, fonds français 2137), which was then adopted by Jean Dufournet in his *La Conquête de Constantinople* (Paris, 2004). Dufournet gives as his reason, "Nous sommes d'accord avec Edmond Faral pour estimer que les manuscripts O et A sont les meilleurs, surtout d'un point de vue historique.

Mais, comme ils ont été pris comme base pour leurs éditions, A par Natalis de Wailly et O par Edmond Faral, notre choix s'est porté sur le manuscrit B, dont nous ne méconnaissons pas les faiblesses, les erreurs et les lacunes: le texte y a été réécrit, en une version plus immédiatement intelligible, et il est intéressant d'étudier cette pratique.

Ce manuscrit a en outre l'avantage d'être sans doute le plus ancien, copiant une version antérieure, et de présenter, comme l'ont écrit les éditeurs du CRAL, 'dans toute la tradition de Villehardouin, le texte linguistiquement le plus homogène en français central', sans influence dialectale. C'est, de ce point de vue, le meilleur témoin" (pp. 34–5).

(We agree with Edmond Faral's judgment that MSS O and A are the best, particularly from a historical perspective. But since they were used as the base texts for their editions, A by Natalis de Wailly and O by Edmond Faral, we chose Manuscript B. We are not unaware of its flaws, errors, and lacunae; the text has been rewritten, in a more immediately intelligible version, and it is interesting to study that process.

This manuscript has the added advantage of being unquestionably the oldest, copying an earlier version, and of offering, to quote the CRAL editors, "in the whole Villehardouin tradition the most linguistically homogeneous in central French," with no dialectal influence. From that point of view it is the best witness.)

After lengthy consideration of these factors and despite the new edition's bonus of an updated bibliography and wealth of supporting information, it seemed preferable in this study to stay with Faral's text not only because of the superiority of its base manuscript (O) but also because the MS B rewrite produced such a flattening effect on the text. Fortunately Dufournet has retained Faral's paragraph numbers, and readers will therefore have no difficulty locating references, whatever edition they choose to use.

6 *La Conquête de Constantinople* (Paris, 1924).
7 *Li Fet des Romains* (Paris, 1938).
8 This fact appears to have escaped the attention of Elisabeth Gauchier in *La Biographie chevaleresque: Typologie d'un genre (xiiie-xve siècles)*.
9 Maria Wyke, *Caesar. A Life in Western Culture*, p. 2.
10 For the Latin tradition of *compilatio*, see A.J. Minnis, *Medieval Theory of Authorship*.
11 "Some Principles of Rhetorical Historiography in the Twelfth Century," p. 103.
12 Isidore of Seville, *Etymologiae*, I, xli–xliv.
13 All translations are my own unless indicated otherwise.
14 See Jeanette Beer, *Narrative Conventions of Truth in the Middle Ages*.

15 Although Isidore cannot provide an adequate working model for modern historians, it is interesting that modern technology may be in the process of reinvigorating and revalidating eyewitness testimony. *The New York Times* (15 April 2010) reports that the Library of Congress will archive the collected works of Twitter, which declares, "it is very exciting that tweets are becoming part of history." It remains to be seen whether the subject matter of such "history" will be "memoria dignum" (worthy of memory).

16 Suzanne Fleischman, "Tense and Narrativity: From Medieval Performance to Modern Fiction," p. 9.

17 For medieval attitudes to the *auctores*, see A.J. Minnis, *Medieval Theory of Authorship*, and for a discussion of the historical intersection of hermeneutical practice and rhetorical theory, see Rita Copeland, *Hermeneutics and Translation in the Middle Ages*.

18 Free indirect speech is sometimes now labelled "le style indirect libre" and is erroneously attributed to Flaubert as a nineteenth-century invention. This variant manner of speech reporting, which blends the characteristics of direct speech with those of indirect speech, was well known to medieval narrators.

1. The First Words of French: Nithard's *Historiae De Dissensionibus Filiorum Ludovici Pii*

1 They are now called "the Strasbourg Oaths," for the place where they were sworn.

2 Gerhard Rohlfs, *From Vulgar Latin to Old French*, p. 69.

3 Nithard was the illegitimate son of Angilbert and Berthe, the daughter of Charlemagne.

4 In chapter 9 ("Public *Histories* and Private History in the Work of Nithard") of her *Politics and Ritual in Early Medieval Europe*, Janet Nelson hypothesizes convincingly that Nithard's private life experiences were at odds with the public histories he had been asked to write by his young cousin Charles the Bald. This is a new approach to the *Histories*, which, she suggests, need reappraisal.

5 For the creation of the Carolingian dynasty and its narrative representations after Charlemagne's death, see Rosamond McKitterick, *Charlemagne: The Formation of a European Identity*.

6 If one excludes the various oaths at Strasbourg, there are only three other such instances in the *Histories*. Quotations from classical sources are also remarkable by their absence, although some readers have claimed to see traces of Virgil, Sallust, Tacitus, and several other *auctores*. The most likely

explanation for these echoes, if echoes they are, is that they emerge from Nithard's stock of memories drawn from a phrase book memorized when he acquired Latin in the palace. When is a quote not a quote?

7 "Nithard … felt cheated and saw Charles's abandonment of the Meuse line as a sad turning point in the negotiations and a consequence of 'trickery.' For it was in this disputed region between the Meuse and the Scheldt, surely, that Nithard's own lost honors lay: lands which (among others) Lothar maintained were indispensable to 'rewarding his faithful followers' … [H]e seems in the early summer [of 842] to have felt still confident of permanent restitution, for he welcomed Lothar's opening of talks with Charles and Louis. But then Lothar wrested the concession that took his western frontier up to the Charbonnière" ("Public *Histories*," pp. 222–3).

8 In one of his occasional mistakes, Nithard conflates this oath with the oath Judith swore on her previous return to court in 831. See Lauer's note in Nithard, *Historiarum Libri IV*, p. 20n1.

9 This text has been emended with the help of A. Ewert's suggestions. For his discussion of problematic areas, see notes 12 and 13 below.

10 The next few paragraphs about the preparation of oaths are adapted from Jeanette Beer, *Early Prose in France*, pp. 16–18.

11 See A. Tabachovitz, *Étude sur la langue de la version française des Serments de Strasbourg*, p. 14.

12 Alfred Ewert, "The Strassburg Oaths," pp. 16–35.

13 For example: "In the French Oaths we have the awkward repetition of *salvar* (l. 6), we have the addition of the phrase *et in ajudha et in cadhuna cosa* (l. 5), which comes oddly after *salvarai*, however we may try to justify its presence, and we have finally, apart from minor blemishes, the crucial passage *de suo part ñ lostanit* (l. 13). Many ingenious explanations and emendations have been suggested for the last two words (*ñ lostanit*), but nothing can alter the fact that the whole phrase is unsatisfactory and suspect … I would … call attention to the violence done to the natural parallelism, which is preserved in the German version: 'If Charles keeps the oath … and Louis breaks it.' In the French version we have neither 'If Louis keeps the oath … and Charles breaks it' nor 'If Louis keeps the oath … and Charles does not keep it,' but 'If Louis keeps the oath … and Charles does not observe it,' that is, a change of verb so unnecessary, so incongruous, and so contrary to notarial habit, that it may well arouse, even in the non-legal mind, a suspicion of some ulterior motive or fraudulent intent" ("The Strassburg Oaths," pp. 20–1).

14 See Muller, "When Did Latin Cease to Be a Spoken Language in France?"

15 See Lot, "A quelle époque a-t-on cessé de parler latin?"

16 See Richter, "A quelle époque a-t-on cessé de parler Latin en Gaule? A propos d'une question mal posée."

17 Roger Wright, *Late Latin and Early Romance in Spain and Carolingian France*, p. 123.

18 For the *correctio* and *emendatio* that were guiding principles in the Carolingian Renaissance, see Rosamond McKitterick, "Royal Patronage of Culture," pp. 117–18.

19 *Annales regni francorum unde ab. A. 741 usque ad a. 829, qui dicuntur Annales laurissenses maiores et Einhardi*, ed. F. Kurze, p. 98.

20 Angilbert died on 18 February 814.

2. Whose Words Are They?: *Gesta Francorum et aliorum Hierosolimitanorum*

1 Bohemond of Taranto (*ca.* 1057–1111) was the eldest son of Robert Guiscard, one of the sons of Tancred de Hauteville, who in 1059 had been confirmed in possession of the duchy of Apulia, and had then attempted to win Durazzo from the Greeks. Bohemond early became a leader in his father's mercenary army, and fought with him against the Greeks until his father's death in 1085. In 1096, Bohemond responded to Pope Urban's call for Christians to rescue the Holy Sepulchre. He led a band of Norman Italian Crusaders from Constantinople to Antioch. That city fell with the help of Firouz, one of the Turkish commanders of the city, on 2 June 1098, and Bohemond claimed it by right of conquest.

2 In 1928, it was suggested (by August Krey, see this volume, pp. 30–1) that a part of the *Gesta Francorum* that was particularly favourable to Bohemond had been modified as propaganda for Bohemond's 1107 campaign against the Byzantine emperor Alexius. This unlikely suggestion, with its anachronistic assumption that medieval historical narratives would be useful in effecting the same political outcomes that we have come to expect from modern media propaganda, is usefully discussed – and dismissed – by Nicholas L. Paul in "A Warlord's Wisdom: Literacy and Propaganda at the Time of the First Crusade."

3 Tancred Marchisus (*ca.* 1076–1112) was the nephew of Bohemond, who persuaded him to take the cross. He accompanied Bohemond to Constantinople in 1096, but avoided taking the oath of allegiance that the other Crusading leaders swore to Alexius I. After the capture of Nicaea, however, he paid homage to the Greek emperor. A daring mercenary with territorial

ambitions, he captured Tarsus but was forced to relinquish it to Baldwin of Boulogne. He became prince of Galilee, was twice his uncle's regent in Antioch, and campaigned successfully several times against the Turks in north Syria. He died of an illness in Antioch on 11 December 1112.

4 Raymond IV de Saint-Gilles (1041/2–1105), Marquis of Provence, was the first of the princes of Western Europe to take the cross (in October 1096). He refused at first to do homage to Alexius I, but later became a firm supporter of the Latin-Greek alliance. Unlike Bohemond, who claimed Antioch as his by right of conquest, Raymond urged that the city be restored to the Greeks. After the fall of Antioch and his expulsion from that city by Bohemond, Raymond became the true leader of the Crusade, and organized a Crusading band (which included our Anonymous) to continue on to Jerusalem. He was the only Crusading leader who conquered no principality in Syria.

5 For the idea that Jerusalem represented the legitimate completion of the *iter* (journey) in a campaign for which there was no formal ending, see E.O. Blake, "The Formation of the 'Crusade Idea,'" pp. 20–1.

6 Hill, p. xviin1.

7 Cf. Paul Fussell, *The Great War and Modern Memory*, pp. 69–71.

8 "Burgus" (outskirts of a town); "casale" (piece of land); "deliberare" (free); "descendere" (dismount from a horse); "Lombardi et Longobardi" (north and south Italians); "merulae" (battlements, in the Bongars edition); "piscine" (drain, sewer); "tenda" (tent, in the Bongars edition), "papilio" (tent); "saumarius" (pack animal). For a detailed study of the *Gesta*'s vocabulary, and stylistic devices see H. Oehler, "Studien zu den *Gesta Francorum*," pp. 58–97.

9 "His narrative is close to that of vernacular culture. In a real if limited sense, the *Gesta Francorum* is a *chanson de geste*. We know that the First Crusade generated vernacular narrative songs ... Anon, like many composers of chanson, like for that matter Villehardouin at the time of the Fourth Crusade, had a strong preference for the dramatic encounter of speakers in confrontation." Colin Morris, "The *Gesta Francorum* as Narrative History," pp. 61–2.

10 See E.R. Curtius, *European Literature and the Latin Middle Ages*, pp. 83–5 and 159–62.

11 Curtius notes that from the time of Homer onwards, there have been examples of this topos in all ages. "In panegyric, the orator finds no words which can fitly praise the person celebrated. It is a standard topos in the eulogy of rulers ... The Middle Ages, in turn, multiplies the names of famous authors who would be unequal to the subject. Included among the

'inexpressibility topos' is the author's assurance that he sets down only a small part of what he has to say" (pp. 159–60).

12 "[N]escio quis compilator, nomine suppresso, libellum super hac re nimis rusticanum ediderat" (Some unknown compiler or other whose name has been suppressed had produced an excessively rustic little book on the subject), *Historia Jerosolimitana, Recueil des Historiens des Croisades Occidentaux* IV, p. 9.

13 Direct speech occurs on pages 2, 4 (two), 6, 18 (two), 24 (two), 42, 44, 46, 48, 52, 54, 58 (three), 70, 72, 76, 78 (two), 80, 82 (four), 84, 88 (three), 98 (two), 100 (two), 102 (three), 104 (three), 106 (three), 112 (four), 114 (three), 116 (three), 118 (five), 120 (two), 122 (two), 124 (five), 126, 128–30, 134 (four), 136 (four), 140, 142 (two), 144 (three), 146, 148 (three), 152, 158 (three), 166, 168, 170, 198, 204, 208, 216.

14 Renderings vary slightly when later chroniclers rehandle the scene. Other formulations are "Deus le vult," "Deus volt," "Deus vult," "Deus id vult," "Deus hoc vult," "Diex le viaut," "Deus id vult." For specific references, see Benoît Lacroix, *"Deus le volt!*: la théologie d'un cri," p. 463.

15 This translation is from *The Authorized Version of the Bible*, Matthew 16:24.

16 The occasion was the Council of Clermont, although Anonymous does not name the council specifically.

17 Robertus Monachus, Sermo Apologeticus, *Historia Iherosolomitana, Recueil des Historiens des Croisades Occidentaux*, Vol. III, 717–882, p. 721.

18 *Recueil des Historiens des Croisades Occidentaux*, Vol. III, p. 729.

19 *Recueil*, Vol. IV, p. 15.

20 *Recueil*, Vol. IV, p. 137.

21 In *American Historical Review* 11, no. 2 (January, 1905), p. 242.

22 *Councils of Urban II, Vol. 1*, and "Clermont 1095; Crusades and Canons," pp. 63–77. The following short bibliography (courtesy of Louis Hamilton, an associate of the Columbia Medieval Seminar) is included for readers wishing to explore the subject further: Alfons Becker, *Papst Urban II (1088–1099)* (Stuttgart, 1964), *MGH*, Schriften 19, vols. 1–2; P.J. Cole, *The Preaching of the Crusades in the Holy Land*, 1095–1270 (Cambridge, MA, 1991); Giles Constable, *Crusaders and Crusading in the Twelfth Century* (Aldershot, Hants, 2008); Carl Erdmann, *The Origin of the Idea of the Crusade*, trans. Walter Goffart and M.W. Baldwin (Princeton, NJ, 1977); Dominique Iogna-Prat, *Order and Exclusion: Cluny and Christendom face Heresy, Judaism, and Islam (1100–1150)*, trans. Graham Robert Edwards (Ithaca, NY, 2002); A. Linder, *Raising Arms: Liturgy in the Struggle to Liberate Jerusalem in the Late Middle Ages* (Turnhout, 2003); G.A. Loud, *The Age of Robert Guiscard:*

Southern Italy and the Norman Conquest (Harlow, 2000); Jonathan Phillips, *The Second Crusade: Expanding the Frontiers of Christendom* (New Haven, CT, 2007); Jay Rubenstein, *Guibert of Nogent: Portrait of a Medieval Mind* (New York, 2002); Carl Servatus, *Paschal II (1099–1118), Studien zu Seiner Person und Seiner Politik, Päpste und Papsttum* 14 (Stuttgart, 1979).

23 See Giles Constable, "Charter Evidence for Pope Urban II's Preaching of the First Crusade," pp. 228–32.

24 *The First Crusade and the Idea of Crusading*, p. 15.

25 Its inspiration is Revelation 6:10.

26 Armelle Leclercq in *Portraits croisés: L'image des Francs et des Musulmans dans les textes sur la Première Croisade* (Paris, 2010) finds striking similarities in the Frankish and Muslim presentation of the First Crusade: "Les mêmes moyens techniques sont employés pour dévaloriser la religion adverse et promouvoir les valeurs de la 'bonne' religion. Cette symétrie intellectuelle est favorisée par la convergence des deux civilisations vers l'idéologie de la guerre sainte" (The same technical means are used to devalorise the opposing religion and to promote the values of the "good" religion. This intellectual symmetry is favored by the convergence of the two civilizations in the direction of holy war, pp. 27–8).

27 Cf. Nithard's *Histories*, where it is the primary inspiration for the literary quotations.

28 Kerbogha ("Karbuqa"/"Courbaran") (d. between 26 October 1101 and 14 October 1102) was emir of Mosul and commander-in-chief of the army of the Sultan of Persia, who sent him to quash the Crusade. He arrived two days too late to save Antioch from Bohemond and the Crusading army.

29 Godefroi de Bouillon, *ca.* 1060–1100, began his Crusading march with his brothers Eustace and Baldwin (the future Baldwin I) in August 1096. His relations with Alexius were uneasy at the beginning, but he was eventually persuaded to swear an oath of allegiance to the emperor in April 1097. When Raymond of Toulouse refused to accept the office of ruler of Jerusalem, Godfrey was elected its first ruler, refusing the title of king, but opting for "advocate of the Holy Sepulchre."

30 Baldwin I, 1058–1118, brother of Godfrey of Bouillon, left for the First Crusade with Godfrey in 1096. He captured Edessa in 1098, was count of Edessa from 1098 to 1100, then king of Jerusalem from 1100 to 1118.

31 Anna Comnena, *The Alexiad*, pp. 343–4.

32 August C. Krey, "A Neglected Passage in the *Gesta* and its Bearing on the Literature of the First Crusade," pp. 77–8. The passage in question is:

> Forsitan adhuc a nostris majoribus sepe delusi erimus; ad ultimum quid facturi erunt? Dicent quoniam, necessitate compulsi, volentes nolentesque humiliaverunt se ad nequissimi imperatoris voluntatem!

Fortissimo autem viro Boamundo, quem valde timebat, quia eum sepe
cum suo exercitu ejecerat de campo, dixit quoniam, si libenter ei juraret,
xv dies eundi terre in extensione ab Antiochia retro daret et viii in latitu-
dine; eique tali modo juravit ut, si ille fideliter teneret illud sacramentum,
iste suum nunquam preteriret. – Tam fortes et tam duri milites, cur hoc
fecerunt? Propterea igitur qui multa coacti erant necessitate. (p. 30)

(Perhaps yet again we shall be deceived by our leaders; in the end what
will they do? They will say that, constrained by necessity, willy-nilly they
bowed to the will of the infamous emperor! To the brave Bohemond,
whom he very much feared, because he had often ejected him and his
army from the battlefield, he said that, if he would willingly commit to
him, he would grant him outside Antioch a territory 15 days' march in
length and eight in breadth; he swore that if he kept that oath faithfully,
he would never renege on his. – Why did soldiers of such strength and
endurance do this? Because they were forced by dire necessity.)

33 "A Warlord's Wisdom: Literacy and Propaganda at the Time of the First
   Crusade": "[The fact that] this period saw a period of historical writing
   created for the purposes of persuasion, does not mean that we should
   assume that these historical narratives would be useful in effecting
   political outcomes in the manner we have come to expect from modern
   propaganda. While historical narrative was a powerful medium through
   which communities such as the abbeys of Fleury and Saint-Denis might
   express a collective identity and attempt to shape wider social memory, a
   charismatic personal presence, a well-crafted story, and a carefully staged
   performance were the tools with which a wise warlord harnessed popular
   support" (pp. 565–6).
34 "Der geographische Exkurs in den lateinischen Geschichtequellen des
   Mittelalters," pp. 192–224.
35 "Le problème de l'auteur des Gesta Francorum et aliorum
   Hierosolimitanorum."
36 Anonymous has a fondness for rhythmic cursus endings at the end
   of a sentence. See Hans Oehler, "Studien zu den 'Gesta Francorum,'"
   pp. 67–71.
37 See Paul Bancourt, Les Musulmans dans les chansons de geste du cycle du Roi.
38 "Le fond même de ce dialogue est tout à fait vraisemblable et a pu être
   connu par des espions" (p. 113n5). (The content of this dialogue is completely credible and could have been known through spies.)
39 Bréhier's distinction between "history" and "literature" is not his alone.
   In his article "The Use of the Anonymous Gesta Francorum in the Early

Twelfth-Century Sources for the First Crusade," John France writes, "There is always a strong reason to suspect the *Gesta*: the literary passages, some quite long, clash with the notion of the direct and straightforward work of a simple knight, and the blandness of Book X is highly suspicious." However, France concludes that "[r]easonable explanations can be found." He also point outs that "the literary passages occur in the accounts of all those who made extensive use of the work," and that his computer analysis of Book X and one of the literary passages to see if separate authorship could be established was inconclusive (p. 30).

40 See p. 303n43.

41 Even the Turkish Kerbogha calls the Greeks "the effeminate race" (p. 148).

42 Anonymous does not mention why eventually he left Bohemond at Antioch to join the Provençal army under Raymond de St-Gilles and continue on to Jerusalem. There is no hint, however, of any personal dissatisfaction with his erstwhile hero. Presumably it was a military decision made by a soldier who felt personally committed to the successful completion of a pilgrimage.

43 John France comments, "The extraordinary popularity of the *Gesta Francorum* in the twelfth century explains why historians have come to treat it as the normal account of the First Crusade. We cannot be certain why it was available to early twelfth-century users, but it clearly was, and their use was multiplied by later generations" ("The Use of the *Gesta Francorum*," p. 36).

3. Villehardouin Who Never to the Best of His Knowledge Spoke an Untrue Word: *La Conquête de Constantinople*

1 Villehardouin, *La Conquête de Constantinople* (Paris, 1938). All references will be to this edition. See pp. 113–4n5 of this volume.

2 For further details of his life, see Jean Longnon, *Recherches sur la vie de Geoffroy de Villehardouin* (Paris, 1939), and Jean Dufournet, *La Conquête de Constantinople*, pp. 10–15 and 353–5.

3 Dufournet calls him "prudhomme" (a worthy man) ("Geoffroy" de Villehardouin, *La Conquête de Constantinople*, p. 29).

4 "Robert de Clari et Villehardouin," pp. 559–64.

5 Edmond Faral, "Villehardouin: la question de sa sincérité."

6 The first part of this chapter on Villehardouin's self-referencing is adapted from Jeanette Beer, "Author-Formulae and the Differentiation of Material in Villehardouin's *La Conquête de Constantinople*."

7 Unless otherwise noted, parenthetical numbers in this chapter refer to paragraph numbers.

8 For example, "et alii plures quorum nomina ignoro" (and many others whose names I do not know) in the *Gesta Francorum et aliorum Hierosolimitanorum*, p. 48 and passim.

9 Examples are numerous from p. 229 onwards.

10 For example, Marie de France's "Sulum la lettre des escriz,/Vus musterai de une suriz." (In accordance with the written word,/I shall tell you of a mouse) at the beginning of the fable "De la suriz et de la reine."

11 *La Conquête de Constantinople*, p. 9n4.

12 "Enqui se croisa Oedes … et maintes bones genz dont li non ne sunt mie en escrit" (Here Odo took the cross … and many fine men whose names are not on record, p. 45).

13 5, 6, 7, 8, 54, 99, 114, 129, 141, 231, 236, 345, 361, 367, 376, 409, 464.

14 *Institutio oratoria* X, 1, 31.

15 Faral gives the full document in an appendix, pp. 215–17.

16 Innocent III, *Epistolae* VI, 99 in Migne, *Patrologiae Latinae* CCVX, 104. For further details, see Queller, *The Fourth Crusade*, p. 78.

17 A useful analysis of free indirect speech in other genres of medieval literature that predate *La Conquête de Constantinople* is provided by Sophie Marnette's "Réflexions sur le discours indirect libre en français medieval."

18 "Sachiez," apostrophe; "terre" … "terre" and "perdissiens," … "perdre," repetition; "granz et large" … "povre et diseteus" and "mult grant plenté de la gent el païs" … "mult avons poi de gent," antithesis. (Some of this analysis of Villehardouin's direct speech is adapted from Beer, *Villehardouin: Epic Historian*, chapter 7.)

19 It is worth observing, however, that even in speech passages, Villehardouin never taxes the patience of his public with excessive length. Sainte-Beuve, an early fan of Villehardouin, judged that the marshal "par instinct et dès le début, était [plus] dans la ligne directe et dans le vrai sens de la future construction française et de sa brièveté définitive" (instinctively and from the beginning he was a direct forerunner in the true direction the French of the future and its definitive brevity). See "Geoffroy de Villehardouin," p. 412.

20 The full text of paras. 143–4 is:

> Et li messages estoit devant les barons en estant et parla: "Seignor, fait il, l'emperere Alexis vos mande que bien set que vos iestes la meillor gent qui soient sanz corone et de la meillor terre qui soit, et mult se mervoille

por quoi ne a quoi vos iestes venu en sa terre ne en son regne: que vos
estes crestïen et il est crestïens, et bien set que vos iestes meü por la
sainte terre d'oltremer et por la sainte croiz et por le sepulcre rescore. Se
vos iestes povres ne disetels, il vos donra volentiers de ses vïandes e de
son avoir, et vos li vuidiez sa terre. Ne vos voldroit autre mal faire, et
ne porquant s'enna il le pooir: car, se vos estiez .xx. tant de gent, ne vos
en porroiz vos aler, se il mal vos voloit faire, que vos ne fuissiez mort
et desconfit."

Par l'acort et par le conseil haus autres barons et le duc de Venise se
leva en piez Coenes de Bethune, qui ere bons chevaliers et sages et bien
eloquens; et respont al message: "Bels sire, vos nos avez dit que vostre
sires se merveille mult por quoi nostre seignor et nostre baron sont entré
en son regne ne en sa terre. En son regne ne en sa terre il ne sont mie entré; quar il le tient a tort et a pechié contre Dieu et contre raison, ainz est
son neveu, qui ci siet entre nos sor une chaiere, qui est fils de son frere
l'empereor Sursac. Mes s'il voloit a la merci son nevou venir et li rendoit
la corone et l'empire, nos li proieriens que il li perdonast et li donast tant
que il peüst vivre richement. Et se vos por cestui message n'i revenez
altre foiz, ne soiez si hardiz que vos plus i revegniez."

(The messenger stood before the barons and said: "My lords, the emperor
Alexius wants you to know that he is fully aware that you are the best
of the uncrowned nobles and you come from the best land in the world,
and he wonders very much for what and to do what you have come to
his country and to his kingdom: for you are Christian and he is Christian,
and he is well aware that you set out to rescue the Holy Land across the
sea and the Holy Cross and the Sepulchre. If you are in poverty and need,
he will willingly give you some of his provisions and his money, provided
you leave his land. He would not otherwise wish to do you harm, and
yet he has the power to do so: for even if you were 20 times as many in
number, if he wished to do you harm, you will not be able to depart with
death and defeat."

By the agreement and advice of the other barons and the doge of Venice, Conon de Béthune, who was a fine knight, wise and very eloquent,
got to his feet; and he responds to the messenger: "Fine sir, you have
told us that your lord wonders very much why our lords and our barons
have come to his kingdom and to his country. They have not come to
his kingdom and to his country; for he possesses it wrongly and sinfully
in defiance of God and reason, it belongs rather to his nephew, who is
seated on a throne among us, and is the son of his brother, the emperor

Isaac. But if he were willing to surrender to the mercy of his nephew and restore the crown and empire to him, we would entreat him to pardon him and donate to him the wherewithal to live in luxury. And unless you return on account of this message, do not be so bold as to return ever again."

21 "Les Discours dans la Chronique de Villehardouin," p. 53.

22 In fact, the abbé had already (para. 83) expressed bluntly in direct speech his opinion on the doge's plan to attack Zara. The abbé's opposition to attacking Christian cities is therefore now clear, and it would be expecting an excess of zeal on Villehardouin's part to highlight the opposition's view twice in the space of ten paragraphs. The Boniface-Baldwin debate (paras. 276–7) is more pertinent, since there the emperor gives no direct statement of his case. (Villehardouin's personal preference is known: it was Boniface, not Baldwin, who was Villehardouin's preferred candidate for the position of emperor.)

23 For example, the unpopularity of the decision to divert the expedition away from Jerusalem to Constantinople leads to a defection that elicits profound dismay in the leaders. Villehardouin's direct speech presentation in para. 115 makes this explicit: "Et quant ce oït li marchis de Monferrat, et li cuens Baudoins de Flandres, et li cuens Loeÿs, et li cuens de Saint Pol, et li baron qui se tenoient a lor acort, si furent mult esmaié et distrent: 'Seignor, nos sommes mal bailli: se ceste gent se partent de nos avec cels qui s'en sont parti par maintes foiz, nostre ost sera failie et nos ne porrons nulle conqueste faire. Mais alons a cels et lor crions merci que il aient por Dieu pitié d'els et de nos, et que il ne se honissent, et que il ne toillent la rescosse d'oltremer.'" (And when the marquis of Montferrat, count Baldwin of Flanders, count Louis, the count of Saint-Pol, and the barons who were of the same mind heard this, they were very dismayed and said: "My lords, we are in real trouble: if, in addition to those who have left on several occasions, these men leave us, our expedition will be ruined and we shall not be able to make any conquest. Let us rather go to them and beg them that for God's sake they have pity on them and us, not dishonor themselves, and not impede the overseas rescue.") Robert de Clari's presents the same dismay but distributes the direct speech differently. See this volume, pp. 63–6.

24 Donald E. Queller, *The Fourth Crusade: The Conquest of Constantinople*, p. 16.

25 It is noteworthy that neither the Crusading author of the *Gesta Francorum* nor Villehardouin's Crusading contemporary Robert de Clari (see chapter 5) found it necessary to begin with a prologue explaining their reasons for writing.

26 Robert de Clari, para. XIV. See this volume, pp. 63–4.
27 Donald E. Queller, Thomas K. Compton, and Donald A. Campbell, "The Fourth Crusade: The Neglected Majority."

4. In the Words of the Poor Knight Robert de Clari: *La Conquête de Constantinople*

1 See George Boudon, "Robert de Clari en Aminois," pp. 702–12 and 734.
2 H. Dusevel, ed., *Histoire abrégée du trésor de l'abbaye royale de St. Pierre de Corbie.*
3 *La Conquête de Constantinople*, ed. Philippe Lauer.
4 He is called "the first known French mémorialiste" in Peter Dembowski, *La Chronique de Robert de Clari* (dustjacket).
5 The vivid excitement of this passage is heightened by Robert's intermingling of past and present tenses (kept in my translation here) as he relives and recreates the scene in his narrative.
6 "Je" occurs in "chist que je vous nomme ichi" (para. I, line 57; Those whom I name for you here), "apparellies si comme je vous ai chi conté" (para. XLIV, lines 42–3; prepared as I have told you here), "ches quatre batalles, que je vous ai chi nommees par devant" (para. XLV, lines 25–6; those four battalions which I named for you before), "si faitement comme je vous ai dit" (para. LV, line 2; as I have told you), "si povre com jou vous ai par devant dit" (para. LXIV, line 3; as impoverished as I told you above), "qui si estoit bele et rike com je vous ai dit" (para. LXVI, lines 68–9; as beautiful and rich as I have told you), "ne je ne quit mie, au mien ensient, que es quarante plus rikes chités du monde eust tant d'avoir comme on trova u cors de Constantinoble" (para. LXXXI, lines 13–16; and I do not believe, to the best of my knowledge, that in the forty richest cities in the world there could be as much wealth as there was to be found in the centre of Constantinople), "si males voies com je vos ai dit" (para. LXXXI, lines 30–1; as disgracefully as I have told you), "li pelerin se furent herbergié, si com je vous ai dit" (para. LXXXII, lines 1–2; the Crusaders set up camp as I told you), "estoit li palais de Bouke de Lion si rikes et si fais com je vous dirai" (para. LXXXII lines 4–5; the palace of Boukeleon was as rich and was constructed as I am about to tell you), "tant d'autres rikes saintuaires illuec, ne le vous porroie mie aconter ne dire le verité" (para. LXXXII, lines 34–5; so many other rich sanctuaries there that I could not relate or tell you the truth of it).
7 The first-person plural occurs in para. I, lines 2, 20, 30, 31, 32, 43, 48, 67, 69, 71, 74, 91, 94; para. XVIII, lines 1, 2 ; para. XXIX, line 7; para. XXX, line 2; para. XXXIII, lines 24, 25; para. XXXIX, line 5; para. LII, line 33;

para. LXV, line 20; para. LXVI, 1; para. LXXXI, line 34; para. LXXXIII, line 6; para. LXXXV, line 27; para. XCII, lines 26, 37; para. CVI, line 1; para. CXII, line 24. The first-person possessive adjective "no," which Robert uses for collective actions of his fellow Crusaders in "no gent," (para. XLVII, line 24), "des noes" (para. XLVII, line 75), and "nos gens" (para. LXVI, line 28), is omitted from consideration here.

 8 In an early-twentieth-century dissertation, E. Wanner argued that Robert dictated his history in 1207 and, when he heard the story, inserted it immediately – but in the wrong place. See E. Wanner, "Robert de Clari, ein altfranzösischer Chronist des IV. Kreuzzuges," pp. 77 ff. Later scholars tend to the view that Robert composed his work shortly after 1216, treating events after his return home fairly summarily.

 9 A detailed account of the legend can be found in *Oeuvres de Rigord et de Guillaume le Breton, historiens de Philippe Auguste*, vol. 1, chapters 37 and 38.

10 One may discount a passing reference to the legendary heroes Alexander and Charlemagne when he describes the booty plundered from Constantinople: "puis que chis siecles fu estorés, si grans avoirs, ne si nobles, ne si rikes, ne fu veus, ne conquis, ne au tans Alixandre, ne au tans Charlemaine" (para. LXXXI, lines 10–13; never since this world began was such great, such fine, such rich wealth ever seen or won, either in the time of Alexander or of Charlemagne).

11 This hymn, thought to have been written by Rabanus Maurus in the ninth century, is still sung on solemn occasions, for example, a coronation, the ordering of priests, or the consecration of bishops.

12 It is noteworthy that at the time Robert was writing *La Conquête de Constantinople*, these comic genres brimming with bourgeois realism were at the peak of their popularity in Robert's native Picardy.

13 Aleaumes: para. LXXVI, lines 15–17.
   Alexius: para. XXXIII, line 83; para. LVIII, lines 13–16; para. LIX, lines 26–7.
   Andronicus: para. XXV, lines 8–9; para. XXV, line 15; para. XXV, lines 48–9.
   Andronicus's steward: para. XXVI, lines 86–7.
   Andronicus's men: para. XXV, lines 11–13.
   Barons: para. IV, lines 3–11; para. LII, lines 27–40; para. LIV, line 13; para. LXII, lines 26–7; para. CXVI, lines 32–4.
   Batallion of the count of St. Pol and Pierre d'Amiens: para. XLVII, lines 44–6.
   Bishop of Soissons: para. XCV, lines 17–24.
   Citizens in Constantinople: para. XXII, line 24; para. XXV, lines 79–80.
   Cry circulating: para. LVII, lines 1–11.

Doge of Venice: para. VI, line 25–34; para. XI, lines 26–8; para. XI, lines 37–49; para. XII, lines 12–21; para. XII, lines 24–30; para. XIII, lines 1–13; para. XIV, lines 8–11; para. XIV, lines 24–26; para. XVII, lines 3–8; para. XXXIII, lines 3–5; para. XLI, lines 14–19; para. LIX, lines 22–6; para. LIX, lines 27–31; para. XCIII, lines 13–25; para. CIX, lines 12–17.

Eustace of Canteleux: para. XLVII, line 61.

Factions in the army: para. XXXIII, lines 7–12; para. XXXIII, lines 12–20.

French: para. XLIX, lines 9–11; para. XLIX, lines 13–16; para. LXVI, lines 35–7.

French army: para. XLVII, lines 64–70.

Genoese: para. XXXVI, lines 12–13; para. XXXVI, line 14–31.

Golden Mantle statues: para. LXXXVIII,lines 9–11.

Greeks: para. XVIII, lines 20–1; para. XXII, lines 26–7; para. LXVI, lines 81–2.

Henry of Flanders: para. XLVII, lines 28–34.

Henry of Flanders' knights: para. XLVIII, lines 4–7.

Innkeeper's wife: para. XXV, lines 28–9.

Isaac: para. XXI, line 83; para. XXII, lines 10–13; para. XXIV, lines 8–14; para. XXV, lines 43–7; para. XXV, lines 53–7; para. LIV, lines 12–13 and 14–15.

Jesus: para. LXXXIII, lines 12–13.

John of Wallachia and high men: para. CVI, lines 23–8.

King of Jerusalem: para. XXXIV, lines 9–10; para. XXXIV, lines 30–1.

King of Jerusalem's sergeants: para. XXXIV, lines 26–7.

Knights and young *bacheliers* in the army: para. CV, lines 11–17.

Manuel: para. XVIII, lines 15–18; para. XVIII, lines 27–36; para. XVIII, line 44; para. XVIII, lines 58–60; para. XVIII, lines 67–8 and lines 70–8.

Manuel's advisors: para. XVIII, lines 42–4.

Marquis of Montferrat: para. V, lines 2–4; para. XVII, lines 9–18; para. XXXIII, line 84; para. XXXIV, lines 31–9; para. XXXVI, lines 5–11; para. XXXVI, line 13; para. CI, lines 12–14 and 21–3.

Marquis of Montferrat's wife: para. CI, lines 15–17.

Messengers to Andronicus: para. XXII, line 59.

Murzuphle: para. LXI, lines 19–22; para. LXVII, lines 7–9; para. LXXI, lines 26–9; para. LXIV, line 25.

Old man in Constantinople: para. XXXIII, lines 89–93.

"On": para. CVII, lines 20–4; para. CIX, lines 12–17.

Patriarch of Constantinople: para. XXII, lines 32–5.

Pierre d'Amiens; para. LXVII, line 61; para. LXXVII, lines 6-7; para. XVII, lines 6–7; para. CVI, lines , 29–35.

Statues of women in Constantinople: para. XCI, lines 7–8 and 9–10.

Sultan of Konia: para. CII, lines 38–53.

Two of the worthiest and wisest man in the army: para. XLVII, lines 6–7.

Venetians: para. XLIX, lines 5–8.

Wallachian and Coman high men: para. CVI, lines 31–2.

Widow: para. XXI, lines 70–1 and 76–9.

Wise man: para. XXV, lines 64–73; para. CI, lines 23–6.

14 D. E. Queller, review of Roberto di Clari, *La Conquista di Costantinopoli*, p. 720.

15 Robert had no access to official documents to inform his quotation practices, whether he employs direct or indirect quotation. (The stylistic complexities of free indirect speech did not tempt him in his history/story writing.) Even if the *ipsissima verba* of the pope's letter had been available, however, it is unlikely that Robert would have presented those exact words. This is, for Robert, one of the doge's dramatic moments, fully deserving the drama of direct speech. It is not the pope's.

16 Villehardouin makes no mention of this.

17 *Speculum* 87, no. 2 (April 2012): 314.

18 See *Die Register Innnocenz III*, ed. Othmar Hageneder and Anton Haidacher (Graz, 1964), *Reg.* 5, no. 160.

19 Villehardouin is more informed on this incident. The doge was in fact represented by three chosen envoys, while the Crusaders sent Conon of Bethune, Miles of Brabant, and Villehardouin himself – an embassy of six – to challenge the Greeks. Conon was chosen to deliver the challenge, couched according to Villehardouin's dignified version (Villehardouin, *La Conquête de Constantinople*, paras. 211–14) in truly formal – although no less threatening – language.

5. In the Words of the Author: *Li Fet des Romains*: The Gallic War

1 Suetonius, *Vitae Caesarum. The Lives'* 12 books begin with Julius Caesar and end with Domitian.

2 For precise details of Philip Augustus's fortification of Paris, see the section entitled "The Walls of Philip Augustus" in John Baldwin, *Paris, 1200*, pp. 25–30.

3 Lucan, *Bellum civile*, II, lines 75ff.

4 See Robert-Henri Bautier, "Philippe Auguste: La personnalité du roi," pp. 34–5.

5 Bautier translates Philip's *luxuria* selectively as "porté sur les femmes" (prone to womanizing), which would not, however, be totally accurate for Caesar's variable inclinations.

6 William of Newburgh, *Historia rerum anglicarum*, vol. I, p. 353.

7 Yves Lefèvre points out that Conon's personal affiliations (he was a cousin of Baldwin of Hainaut and a faithful supporter of Philip of Flanders) were surely responsible for the Queen Mother's (Adèle of Champagne's) distaste, but that the reasons for her son's discourtesy were probably more complex. At the time of Conon's poetic performance, Philip was in the process of negotiating his marriage to Isabelle of Hainaut. Thus, "Philippe II n'avait pas les mêmes raisons que sa mère de vexer Conon et son sourire probable traduisait peut-être l'amusement qu'il éprouvait à voir l'irritation arrogante de la reine-mère envers le parti des Flamands au moment même où la victoire de celui-ci était assurée par le mariage déjà projetée en cachette" (Philip II had not the same reasons as his mother for annoying Conon and his presumed smile perhaps betrayed his amusement at seeing the Queen Mother's proud irritation toward the Flemish side at the very moment when the latter's victory was assured by the clandestinely arranged marriage) (Yves Lefèvre, "L'Image du roi chez les poètes," p. 138).

8 Conon's complaint is valuable evidence of Francien's advances toward dialectal supremacy in the early thirteenth century, advances that were directly linked with Philip's inexorable rise to power and with Paris's geographic centrality.

9 Lefèvre, p. 138.

10 "La culture historique des nobles: Le succès des Faits des Romains xive-xve siècles," pp. 265–7.

11 Berthe Marti, "Arnulfus and the *Faits des Romains*."

12 *Etymologiae* I, xliii.

13 *B.g.* book V, section 41.

14 The reviewer of a recent translation of *Madame Bovary* lists *le style indirect libre* as one of the hazards that make the translation of Flaubert "a poisoned chalice": "[T]ranslators of *Madame Bovary* … approach it with trepidation in the knowledge that its writerly secrets – the 'free indirect style,' the subtle ironies and the Master's anguished obsession with the *mot juste* – have been widely exposed and cannot be ignored" (David Coward, "Word by Tragic Word," p. 24).

15 Sallust, *Catilina*, 1–2.

16 For a detailed study of the differences between the two prologues and of the intentional anachronism that characterizes his translative practices generally, see Jeanette Beer, A *Medieval Caesar*, pp. 13–26, pp. 94–8, and passim.

17 "The first of his family who obtained a curule office, a man newly ennobled, an upstart"; see Lewis and Short, A *Latin Dictionary*.

18 At the mention of the word "basilisk" during Lucan's digression about the snakes in Egypt, for example, the translator adds this explanation: "Le roi des serpenz l'apele l'Escriture" (p. 608, line 12; Scripture calls it the king of the serpents), "Scripture" here being Isidore's *Etymologiae* XII, 4.

19 For the evolution of paradoxical usages for the truth convention in other French vernacular prose writings, see Jeanette Beer, *Narrative Conventions of Truth in the Middle Ages*.

20 See this volume, p. xii.

21 His explanation is actually a slightly abbreviated translation of Suetonius's original comment that "Pontico triumpho inter pompae fercula trium verborum praetulit titulum VENI-VIDI-VICI non acta bella significantem sicut ceteris, sed celeriter confecti notam" (In the Pontic triumph he show-cased among the items on the float a sign with the three words "I came, I saw, I conquered," not signifying so much the achievements of war, like the other triumphs, but rather the speed with which it was over, *Vitae* book I, para. 37). The translator prefers to avoid unnecessarily mysterious references that would be incomprehensible to his public, and the phrase "sicut ceteris" was just such a reference.

22 Claude Buridant's remark on the problems presented to vernacular translators by the Latin language, "langue d'encodage facile mais de décodage difficile par son haut degré de condensation" (a language whose high degree of concentration makes it easy to encode but difficult to decode), is here pertinent: "formés et informés par une rhétorique d'amplification, les traducteurs médiévaux cherchent spontanément à dé-plier et dénouer cette condensation sur l'axe paradigmatique, horizontal, d'une syntaxe analytique et d'un lexique à dédoublement, au risque de la *surtraduction*, aux yeux des modernes, pour la maîtriser progressivement dans les prémisses de l'humanisme" (formed and informed by a rhetoric of amplification, medieval translators spontaneously seek to open up and loosen this condensation paradigmatically, horizontally, with an analytic syntax and lexical duplication at the risk of *overtranslation*, from a modern perspective, in order progressively to master it within humanistic prem-isses; "Modèles et remodelages," p. 126).

23 *Etymologiae* X, 3, 12–13. For further information on Caesar's birth and rel-evant etymologies, see Flutre and Sneyders de Vogel, Vol. 2, p. 64.

24 This is a misreading of Cumae by the compiler who then glosses his mis-reading of "Cusmo" as "an island."

25 Julius Caesar, *Bellum gallicum*, ed. H.J. Edwards.

26 "Suetoines ne refet fors touchier ses batailles, car Cesar meïsmes en fist livres ou Lucans prist la greignor partie de ce que il en escrist fors

solement de ceste bataille d'Alyssandre" (Suetonius for his part only
touches on his [i.e., Caesar's] battles, for Caesar himself wrote a book on
them from which Lucan took most of what he wrote about them with the
single exception of this battle at Alexandria, p. 652, lines 3–6).

27 See Virginia Brown, "Portraits of Julius Caesar in Later Manuscripts of
the Commentaries," p. 322: "Although Lupus of Ferrières, Aimoinus of
Fleury, William of Malmesbury, Robert of Torigny, Richard of Bury, and the
authors of *Gesta episcoporum Cameracensium* and *Versus de praeconio urbis
Laudunensis* all refer to [Caesar's] authorship of the *Commentaries* (usually
only the *Gallic War*) in at least a general way, their influence was not sufficient to prevent the development of a misconception in the matter. In the
later Middle Ages and the early Renaissance the *Commentaries* were often
attributed to Julius Celsus Constantinus, a mysterious personage whose
name first appears as a corrector (?) in colophons of the ninth-century wit-
nesses of the *Gallic War*. He has been assigned a tentative floruit around
the middle of the fifth century. In Paris, Bibliothèque Nationale lat. 5056
(s. XI/XII) 'legi' is expanded to 'legati' in the colophons to *Gallic War* 1
and 2; during the twelfth century his name crept up into the tituli to the
first book, and so he became a person of some importance. In the fourteenth century Vincent of Beauvais considers Celsus to be the author of
the *Gallic War*. The mistake was current also in the fourteenth century also,
for Boccaccio, Benvenuto Rambaldi da Imola, and particularly Petrarch
believed too that Celsus had composed the *Gallic War*, if not the entire
corpus."

28 The explicit of London, British Museum, Old Royal 17 F II, fol. 353d,
copied at Bruges in 1479 for Edward IV, reads: "Icy fine la grande histoire
Cesar tirée de pluiseurs acteurs comme Lucan, Suetoine, Orose, Saluste, Julius Celsus et autres, laquelle a esté faicte a Bruges du commandement de
tres hault, tres excellent et tres victorieux prince le roy Edouard quatrieme
de ce nom l'an de grace mil .cccc. lxxix" (Here ends the great history of
Caesar drawn from several authors such as Lucan, Suetonius, Orosius, Sallust, Julius Celsus and others, made at Bruges by order of the most noble,
most excellent, most victorious prince, King Edward the Fourth of this
name in the year of grace 1479) (fol. 353 d).

29 Paris, Bibliothèque Nationale, ancien fonds français n° 294 (anc. 6918).

30 603 paragraphs as against Lucan's 293, Suetonius's 121, and Sallust's 60.

31 By comparison, Lucan is named 92 times, Suetonius 26 times, and Sallust
8 times.
   Lucan: 344/9, 344/19, 344/23, 347/1, 347/25, 356/8, 356/15, 358/30,
363/13, 376/4, 377/1, 382/31, 386/24, 389/8, 405/35, 414/5, 421/1,

424/18, 429/25, 431/19, 448/13, 448/31, 449/1, 451/18, 452/33, 458/10,
458/24, 466/23, 471/21, 471/22, 476/1, 481/15, 487/5, 491/11, 493/18,
495/22, 504/20, 510/9, 511/28, 519/2, 519/31, 520/29, 521/8, 521/10,
522/2, 522/12, 537/7, 539/17, 542/31, 543/4, 545/1, 546/21, 553/27,
562/11, 563/30, 566/26, 567/1, 570/5, 570/27, 571/4, 572/6, 572/12,
574/1, 574/4, 574/6, 590/33, 594/29, 596/3, 597/7, 597/17, 600/22,
601/28, 602/11, 603/20. 604/11, 604/11 (i.e., twice in the same line), 614/2,
615/22, 618/15, 621/1, 622/20, 623/17, 624/8, 635/31, 636/19, 637/10,
645/1, 651/27, 651/31, 652/4, 652/28, 654/21.

Suetonius: 55/33, 54/9, 352/26, 357/4, 522/14, 645/3, 652/3, 652/9,
652/19, 652/24, 652/28, 652/32, 653/4, 654/24, 697/27, 711/8, 711/23,
712/7, 716/17, 717/4, 726/29, 729/30, 739/5, 740/16, 740/25, 744/21.

"Julius Celsus" ("Julian," "Julien"): 75/14, 79 (in the title of the Gallic
section), 106/22, 148/18, 184/25, 219/21, 222/24, 222/28, 229/2, 242/14,
252/8, 339/31.

Julius Caesar ("Cesar" when his work is cited by the translator as separate from the above "Celsus"): 522/14, 652/4, 652/6.

Sallust: 21/21, 22/12, 30/17, 36/1, 36/14, 44/11, 45/27, 724/10. (Since
only a limited amount of Sallust's work is used by the translator, the ratio
of occurrences of Sallust's name is proportionately quite high.)

32 The translator mistakes continual night for continual day in his rendering
   "en aucun tens de l'an n'i anuite de .xxx. jors" (at a certain time of the year
   there is no night there for 30 days, p. 184, lines 23–4; my emphasis).

33 "Id eane de causa, quam legatis pronuntiarunt, an perfidia adducti fecerint,
   quod nihil nobis constat, non videtur pro certo esse proponendum"
   (Because it is not clear to us whether they did what they did for the reason
   they stated to the deputies or because they were motivated by treachery, it
   does not seem appropriate to affirm it as a certainty, B.g. VII, 5).

34 It should be noted that the statement beginning "car l'en met …" is not an
   ambiguous example of the free indirect speech that often follows "car" in
   medieval reported speech. In fact, the present tense renders Caesar own
   words: "Id mihi duabus de causis instituisse videntur, quod neque in
   vulgum disciplinam efferri velint neque eos, qui discunt, litteris confisos
   minus memoriae studere: *quod fere plerisque accidit, ut praesidio litterarum
   diligentiam in perdiscendo ac memoriam remittant*" (It seems to me that they
   have instituted this for two reasons, because they do not want the rule to
   be vulgarized, and they do not want those who learn to rely on the written
   word at the expense of cultivating their memory: *because it happens to the
   vast majority of people that by relying on the aid of the written word they slacken
   their diligence and their memory, B.g.* VI, 14; my emphasis). This is an opinion

from which the translator wishes to dissociate himself. To avoid the ambiguity of free indirect speech and to avoid the suggestion that he might be endorsing "Celsus's" opinion, he carefully cites his source here.

35 For details of his Gallic transformations, see Beer, *A Medieval Caesar*, chapter 5 and passim.

36 Cf. the translator's intervention when he uses Lucan's narrative about Marius and a "German man" to ridicule Philip Augustus's enemies, that "crazy alliance of Germans, English, and Normans" (see this volume, pp. 89–90).

6. In the Words of the Author: *Li Fet des Romains:* The Civil War

1 "No Two Snowflakes Are Alike," p. 12.

2 *Etymologiae* I, xl–xliv.

3 Other examples of harsh psychological judgments of Caesar that have been tagged as "Lucan's words" occur on p. 377, line 1; p. 386, line 23; p. 389, line 8; and p. 451, line 18.

4 See, for example, Berthe Marti, "Arnulfus and the *Fets des Romains.*"

5 See p. 123, line 8; p. 132, line 22; p. 254, line 24; p. 330, line 4; p. 376, line 4; p. 409, line 11.

6 This and his earlier expansion of Lucan's treatment of Cleopatra episode (p. 623 ff.) exploit contemporary tastes for romance, being titillating itself while making reproving noises about titillation and *luxuria* (see Beer, *A Medieval Caesar*, chapter 10). It should be noted, however, that any *inventio* on his part concerning Caesar's womanizing is fundamentally disapproving. He is *not* ultimately romancing Caesar's exploits in this area, and his additions (unlike his later epic interpolations on warfare) are cautionary in nature.

7 See Sneyders de Vogel, "Les Vers dans les Faits des Romains."

8 Cicero was not, in fact, present at the battle, but the mistake was Lucan's, not the translator's. See *The Oxford Classical Dictionary* (p. 620): "There are a few glaring departures from historical truth [in Lucan's account of the Civil War], as when [Lucan] makes Cicero, who was not present at Pharsalus, deliver a harangue to Pompey on the eve of the battle."

9 The translator's regional loyalties can be gauged by such anachronisms.

10 Ian Wei, "From Twelfth-century Schools to Thirteenth-century Universities: The Disappearance of Biographical and Autobiographical Representations of Scholars," a lecture delivered to the Medieval Studies Program, Princeton University, 13 April 2010. I thank Dr Wei for providing me with the full text of his lecture, which has since appeared in *Speculum*.

Afterword

1 In *Past Convictions: The Penance of Louis the Pious and The Decline of the Caro-lingians*, Courtney M. Book writes, "It has long been thought that Nithard's work survives in only one manuscript of the late ninth century (Paris, B. N. F. lat. 9768) and in an incomplete copy of this manuscript made in the fifteenth (Paris, B. N. F. lat. 14663). Yet much remain to be said about the transmission and reception of Nithard's text; see C. M. Booker, 'An Early Humanist Edition of Nithard, *De dissensionibus filiorum Ludovici Pii*; Troyes, Médiathèque de l'Agglomération Troyenne, 3203,' *Revue d'histoire des textes* (forthcoming)" (p. 294n136). I mention this reference for completeness, but at the time of writing have not seen the article in question.

2 Madden, p. 329.

Works Cited

Primary Sources

Anna Comnena. *The Alexiad*. Translated by E.R.A. Sewter. London, 1969.

Annales regni francorum unde ab. A. 741 usque ad a. 829, qui dicuntur Annales laurissenses maiores et Einhardi. Vol. 6. Edited by F. Kurze. *Schriften der Monumenta Germaniae Historica*, Hanover, 1895.

The Annals of Saint-Bertin: Ninth-Century Histories. Vol. 1. Translated by Janet L. Nelson. Manchester, 1991.

Baudri de Bourgeuil. *Historia Jerosolimitana. Recueil des Historiens des Croisades Occidentaux*. Vol. IV. Paris, 1841–95.

Biblia Sacra juxta Vulgatam Clementinam, nova editio. Madrid, 1977.

Bible, The Holy. King James Authorized Version. Oxford.

Caesar, Julius. *Bellum Gallicum*. Edited by H.J. Edwards. Cambridge, MA, 1917; reprinted 1970.

Caesar, Julius. *Bellum Gallicum*. Edited by Otto Seel. Leipzig, 1968.

Canso d'Antioca. An Epic Chronicle of the First Crusade. Edited by Carol Sweetenham and Linda M. Paterson. Aldershot, Hants, 2003.

Carolingian Chronicles: Royal Frankish Annals and Nithard's *Histories*. Translated by Bernhard Walter Scholz with Barbara Rogers. Ann Arbor, MI, 1970.

Fet des Romains, Li. Edited by L.-F. Flutre and K. Sneyders de Vogel. 2 vols. Paris, 1938.

Fulcher of Chartres. A *History of the Expedition to Jerusalem 1095–1127*. Translated by F.R. Ryan. Edited and with an introduction by Harold S. Fink. Knoxville, 1969.

Gesta Dei per Francos. Edited by Jacques Bongars. Hanover, 1612.

Gesta Francorum. Anonymi Gesta Francorum et aliorum Hierosolymitanorum. Edited by Beatrice A. Lees. Oxford, 1924.

Gesta Francorum et Aliorum Hierosolimitanorum. The Deeds of the Franks and the Other Pilgrims to Jerusalem. Edited by R.M.T. Hill. London, 1962.

Gesta Francorum et Aliorum Hierosolimitanorum. Edited by Louis Bréhier. Paris, 1964.

Anonymi Gesta Francorum et aliorum Hierosolymitanorum. Edited by Hagenmeyer. Heidelberg, 1890.

Guibert de Nogent. *Gesta Dei per Francos. Recueil des Historiens des Croisades Occidentaux*. Vol. IV. Paris, 1841–95.

Innocent III. *Epistolae*. Edited by J.P. Migne. *Patrologiae Latinae*. Vol. CCXV. Paris, 1855.

Innocent III. *Die Register Innnocenz III*. Edited by Othmar Hageneder and Anton Haidacher. *Reg*. 5, no. 160. Graz, 1964.

Isidore of Seville. *Etymologiarum sive Originum*. Edited by W.M. Lindsay. Oxford, 1911.

Lucan. *Bellum civile*. Cambridge, MA, 1928; reprinted 1969.

Nithard. *Historiarum Libri IV. Histoire des fils de Louis le Pieux*. Edited by P. Lauer. Paris, 1926.

Ovid. *Metamorphoses*. Edited by Frank Justus Miller. Cambridge, MA, 1916; reprinted 1984.

Quintilian. *Institutio oratoria*. Cambridge, 1980.

Rigord. *Histoire de Philippe Auguste*. Edited and translated by Elisabeth Carpentier, Georges Pon, and Yves Chauvin. Paris, 2006.

Rigord. *Oeuvres de Rigord et de Guillaume le Breton, historiens de Philippe Auguste*. Edited by H.-Fr. Delaborde. Paris, 1882.

Robert de Clari. *La Conquête de Constantinople*. Edited by Philippe Lauer. Paris, 1924.

Roberto di Clari. *La conquista di Costantinopoli (1198–1216)*. Edited by Anna Maria Nada Patrone. Genoa, 1972.

Robert de Clari. *The Conquest of Constantinople*. Translated by Edgar Holmes McNeal. New York, 1936; reprinted Toronto, 1999.

Robertus Monachus. *Historia Iherosolomitana, Recueil des Historiens des Croisades Occidentaux*. Vol. III. Paris, 1841–95.

Robert the Monk. *History of the First Crusade*. Translated by Carol Sweetenham. Aldershot, 2005.

Sallust. *Catilina*. Edited by Alphonsus Kurfess. Leipzig, 1968.

Suetonius. *Vitae Caesarum*. Edited by J. C. Rolfe. London, 1913; reprinted 1970.

Villehardouin, Geoffroy de. *La Conquête de Constantinople*. Edited by Edmond Faral. Paris, 1938.

Villehardouin, Geoffroy de. *La Conquête de Constantinople*. Edited by Jean Dufournet. Paris, 2004.

William of Newburgh. *Historia rerum anglicarum. Chronicles and Memorials of the Reigns of Stephen, Henry II and Richard I.* Vol. I. Rolls Series. London, 1884–89.

Secondary Sources

Baldwin, John, W. *Paris, 1200*. Paris, 2006; reprinted Stanford, CA, 2010.
Bancourt, Paul. *Les Musulmans dans les chansons de geste du cycle du Roi*. Aix-en-Provence, 1982.
Bautier, Robert-Henri. "Philippe Auguste: la personnalité du roi." In *La France de Philippe Auguste: Le Temps des mutacions*, 2–57. Edited by Robert-Henri Bautier. Paris, 1982.
Becker, Alfons. *Papst Urban II (1088–1099)*. In *Schriften der Monumenta Germaniae Historica*, Bd. 19, 1–2. Edited by Alfons Becker. Stuttgart, 1964–2012.
Beer, Jeanette. *Villehardouin. Epic Historian*. Geneva, 1968.
Beer, Jeanette. A *Medieval Caesar*. Geneva, 1976.
Beer, Jeanette. "Author-Formulae and the Differentiation of Material in Villehardouin's *La Conquête de Constantinople*." *Romance Philology* 32, no. 3 (1979): 298–302.
Beer, Jeanette. *Narrative Conventions of Truth in the Middle Ages*. Geneva, 1981.
Beer, Jeanette. *Early Prose in France*. Kalamazoo, MI, 1992.
Beer, Jeanette. "Heroic Language and the Eyewitness: The *Gesta Francorum* and *La Chanson d'Antioche*." In *Echoes of the Epic*, 1–16. Edited by David P. Schenck and Mary Jane Schenck. Birmingham, AL, 1998.
Blake, E.O. "The Formation of the 'Crusade Idea.'" *Journal of Ecclesiastical History* 21, no. 1 (January 1970): 11–31.
Booker, Courtney M. *Past Convictions: The Penance of Louis the Pious and The Decline of the Carolingians*. Philadelphia, 2009.
Boudon, Georges. "Robert de Clari en Aminois." *Bulletin de la Société des antiquaires de Picardie* 19 (1895–97): 700–34.
Brown, Virginia. "Portraits of Julius Caesar in Later Manuscripts of the Commentaries." *Viator* 12 (1981): 319–53.
Bull, M.J. "Overlapping and Competing Identities in the Frankish First Crusade." In *Le Concile de Clermont de 1095 et l'Appel à la Croisade: Actes du Colloque à l'Université Internationale à Clermont-Ferrand* (22–25 juin, 1995), 195–211. Edited by A. Vauchez. Rome, 1997.
Buridant, Claude. "Modèles et remodelages." In *Translations médiévales: cinq siècles de traduction en français au Moyen Age (xie-xve siècles)*. Vol. 1. Edited by Claudio Galderisi. Turnhout, Belgium, 2011.
Cole, P.J. *The Preaching of the Crusades in the Holy Land, 1095–1270*. Cambridge, MA, 1991.

Compagnon, Antoine. *La seconde main ou le travail de la citation*. Paris, 1979.

Constable, Giles. *Crusaders and Crusading in the Twelfth Century*. Aldershot, Hants, 2008.

Constable, Giles. "Charter Evidence for Pope Urban II's Preaching of the First Crusade." In *Canon Law, Religion, and Politics. Liber Amicorum Robert Somerville*, 228–32. Edited by Uta-Renate Blumenthal, Anders Winroth, and Peter Landau. Washington, DC, 2012.

Copeland, Rita. *Hermeneutics and Translation in the Middle Ages*. Cambridge, 1991.

Coward, David. "Word by Tragic Word," *Times Literary Review*, 13 April 2012: 24.

Cowdrey, H.E.J. "Pope Urban's Preaching of the First Crusade." *History* 55 (June 1970): 177–88.

Cowdrey, H.E.J. "The Reform Papacy and the Origin of the Crusades." In *Le Concile de Clermont de 1095 et l'Appel à la Croisade. Actes du Colloque Universitaire International de Clermont-Ferrand (23–25 juin, 1995)*, 65–83. Edited by A. Vauchez. Rome, 1997.

Curtius, E.R. *European Literature and the Latin Middle Ages*. Translated by Willard R. Trask. New York, 1953.

Delaborde, H.-Fr., ed. *Oeuvres de Rigord et de Guillaume le Breton, historiens de Philippe Auguste*. Paris, 1882.

Dembowski, Peter. *La Chronique de Robert de Clari*. Toronto, 1963.

Dufournet, Jean. *Villehardouin et Clari*. Paris, 1973.

Erdmann, Carl. *The Origin of the Idea of the Crusade*. Translated by Walter Goffart and M.W. Baldwin. Princeton, NJ, 1977.

Ewert, Alfred. "The Srassburg Oaths." *Transactions of the Philological Society* (1935): 16–35.

Faral, Edmond. "Villehardouin: la question de sa sincérité." *Revue historique* 177 (1936): 530–82.

Fleischman, Suzanne. *Tense and Narrativity: From Medieval Performance to Modern Fiction*. Austin, TX, 1990.

Flutre, L.-F. *Les Manuscrits des* Faits des Romains. Paris, 1932.

Flutre, L.-F. Li Fait des Romains *dans les littératures française et italienne du xiiie au xvie siècle*. Paris, 1932.

Foreville, Raymonde. "L'Image de Philippe dans les sources contemporaines." In *La France de Philippe Auguste: Le Temps des mutacions*, 115–32. Edited by Robert-Henri Bautier. Paris, 1982.

France, John. "The Use of the Anonymous *Gesta Francorum* in the Early Twelfth-Century Sources for the First Crusade." In *From Clermont to Jerusalem. The Crusades and Crusader Societies*, 29–42. Edited by A.W. Murray. Turnhout, Brepols, 1998.

Frappier, Jean. "Les Discours dans la Chronique de Villehardouin." In *Etudes dédiées à Mario Roques*. Paris, 1946.

Fussell, Paul. *The Great War and Modern Memory*. Oxford, 1975.

Gauchier, Elisabeth. *La Biographie chevaleresque: Typologie d'un genre (xiiie-xve siècles)*. Paris, 1994.

Gaunt, Simon, and Sarah Kay, eds. *The Cambridge Companion to Medieval French Literature*. Cambridge, 2008.

Guenée, Bernard. "La culture historique des nobles: Le succès des *Faits des Romains* xive-xve siècles." In *La noblesse au moyen âge. Essais à la mémoire de Robert Bautruche*, 261–88. Edited by Philippe Contamine. Paris, 1976.

Horrent, Jules. "Chroniques latines primitives et chansons de geste espagnoles." In *Mélanges offerts à Edmond-René Labande*, 407–15. Poitiers, 1974.

Iogna-Prat, Dominique. *Order and Exclusion: Cluny and Christendom face Heresy, Judaism, and Islam (1100–1150)*. Translated by Graham Robert Edwards. Ithaca, NY, 2002.

Krey, August C. "A Neglected Passage in the *Gesta* and its Bearing on the Literature of the First Crusade." In *The Crusades and Other Historical Essays Presented to his Former Students by Dana C. Munro*, 57–78. Edited by Louis J. Paetow. New York, 1928.

Lacroix, Benoît. "*Deus le volt!*: la théologie d'un cri." In *Mélanges offerts à Edmond-René Labande*, 461–70. Poitiers, 1974.

Leclercq, Armelle. *Portraits croisés: L'image des Francs et des Musulmans dans les textes sur la première croisade*. Paris, 2010.

Leeker, Joachim. *Die Darstellung Cäsars in den romanischen Literaturen des Mittelalters*. Frankfurt-am-Main, 1986.

Lefèvre, Yves. "L'Image du roi chez les poètes." In *La France de Philippe Auguste: Le Temps des mutacions*, 133–44. Edited by Robert-Henri Bautier. Paris, 1982.

Lewis, Charlton T., and Charles Short. A *Latin Dictionary*. Oxford, 1879; reprinted 1975.

Linder, A. *Raising Arms: Liturgy in the Struggle to Liberate Jerusalem in the Late Middle Ages*. Turnhout, 2003.

Longnon, Jean. *Recherches sur la vie de Geoffroy de Villehardouin*. Paris, 1939.

Longnon, Jean. *Les Compagnons de Villehardouin. Recherches sur les croisés de la quatrième croisade*. Geneva, 1978.

Lot, Ferdinand. "A quelle époque a-t-on cessé de parler latin?" *Archivum Latinitatis Medii Aevi, Bulletin De Cange* 7 (1931): 97–159.

Loud, G.A. *The Age of Robert Guiscard: Southern Italy and the Norman Conquest*. Harlow, 2000.

McKitterick, Rosamond. "Royal Patronage of Culture in the Frankish Kingdoms under the Carolingians: Motives and Consequences." In *The Frankish Kings and Culture in the Early Middle Ages*, Chapter 7. Aldershot, 1995.

McKitterick, Rosamond. *Charlemagne. The Formation of a European Identity*. Cambridge, 2008.

Madden, Thomas, F. "The Venetian Version of the Fourth Crusade: Memory and the Conquest of Constantinople in Medieval Venice." *Speculum* 87, no. 2 (April 2012): 311–44.

Marnette, Sophie. "Réflexions sur le discours indirect libre en français médiéval." *Romania* 114 (1996): 1–49.

Marnette, Sophie. *Speech Thought and Presentation in French: Concepts and Strategies.* Amsterdam, 2005.

Marti, Berthe. "Arnulfus and the *Faits des Romains.*" *Modern Language Quarterly* 2 (1941): 3–23.

Meier, Christian. *Caesar.* Translated by David McClintock. Glasgow, 1995.

Minnis, A.J. *Medieval Theory of Authorship.* London, 1984.

Morris, Colin. "The *Gesta Francorum* as Narrative History." *Reading Medieval Studies* 19 (1993): 55–71.

Munro, Dana C. "The Speech of Pope Urban II at Clermont, 1095." *American Historical Review* 11 (1905–6): 231–42.

Muller, Henry F. "When Did Latin Cease to Be a Spoken Language in France?" *Romanic Review* 12 (1921): 318–34.

Nelson, Janet. *Politics and Ritual in Early Medieval Europe.* London, 1986.

Oehler, Hans. "Studien zu den *Gesta Francorum.*" *Mittellateinisches Jahrbuch* 6 (1970): 58–97.

The Oxford Classical Dictionary. Edited by N.G.L. Hammond and H.H. Scullard. Oxford, 1970.

Paul, Nicholas L. "A Warlord's Wisdom: Literacy and Propaganda at the Time of the First Crusade." *Speculum* 85, no. 3 (July 2010): 534–66.

Pauphilet, A. "Robert de Clari et Villehardouin." In *Mélanges de linguistique et de literature offerts à M. Alfred Jeanroy*, 559–64. Paris, 1928.

Pauphilet, A. "Sur Robert de Clari." *Romania* 57 (1931): 289–311.

Phillips, Jonathan. *The Second Crusade: Expanding the Frontiers of Christendom.* New Haven, CT, 2007.

Queller, Donald E. "Review of Roberto di Clari, *La conquista di Costantinopoli (1198–1216)*, edited by Anna Maria Nada Patrone." *Speculum* 49, no. 4 (October 1974): 719–22.

Queller, Donald E. *The Fourth Crusade. The Conquest of Constantinople, 1201–1204.* Philadelphia, 1977.

Queller, Donald E., Thomas K. Compton, and Donald A. Campbell. "The Fourth Crusade: The Neglected Majority." *Speculum* 49, no. 3 (July 1974): 441–65.

Rabassa, Gregory. "No Two Snowflakes Are Alike." In *The Craft of Translation*, 1–12. Edited by John Biguenet and Rainer Schulte. Chicago, 1989.

Richter, Michael. "A quelle époque a-t-on cessé de parler latin en Gaule? A propos d'une question mal posée." *Annales E.S.C.* 38 (1983): 439–48.

Riley-Smith, Jonathan. *The First Crusade and the Idea of Crusading.* London, 1986.

Riley-Smith, Jonathan. *The First Crusaders, 1095–1131*. Cambridge, 1997.

Riley-Smith, Louise, and Jonathan Riley-Smith. *The Crusades. Idea and Reality 1095–1274*. London, 1981.

Rohlfs, Gerhard. *From Vulgar Latin to Old French*. Translated by Vincent Almazan and Lilian McCarthy. Detroit, 1970.

Rubenstein, Jay. *Guibert of Nogent: Portrait of a Medieval Mind*. New York, 2002.

Sainte-Beuve, C.-A. "Geoffroy de Villehardouin." In *Les Causeries du lundi*, 3rd. ed., Vol. 9, 381–412. Paris, 1866.

Schon, P.M. *Studien zum Stil der frühen französischen Prosa. (Robert de Clari, Geoffroy de Villehardouin, Henri de Valenciennes)*. Frankfurt am Main, 1960.

Servatus, Carl. *Paschal II (1099–1118). Studien zu Seiner Person und Seiner Politik, Päpste und Papsttum* 14. Stuttgart, 1979.

Sneyders de Vogel, K. "Les Vers dans les *Faits des Romains*." In *Mélanges de philologie offerts à Salverda de Grave*. Gröningen, 1933.

Sneyders de Vogel, K. "Recherches sur *Les Faits des Romains*." *Romania* 59 (1933): 41–72.

Somerville, Robert. *Councils of Urban II, Vol. 1: Decreta Claromontensia*. Amsterdam, 1972.

Somerville, Robert. "Clermont 1095: Crusades and Canons." In *La primera Cruzada, novecientos anos despues; El Concilio de Clermont y los origenes del Movimiento Cruzada*, 63–77. Edited by Luis Garcia-Guijarro Ramos. Madrid, 1997.

Tabachovitz, A. *Étude sur la langue de la version française des Serments de Strasbourg*. Uppsala, 1932.

Tolan, John. *Les Sarrasins*. Paris, 2003.

Wanner, E. "Robert de Clari, ein altfranzösischer Chronist des IV Kreuzzuges." PhD diss.,University of Zürich, 1901.

Ward, John O. "Some Principles of Rhetorical Historiography in the Twelfth Century." In *Classical Rhetoric and Medieval Historiography*, 103–65. Edited by Ernst Breisach. Kalamazoo, MI, 1985.

Wei, Ian. "From Twelfth-century Schools to Thirteenth-century Universities: The Disappearance of Biographical and Autobiographical Representations of Scholars." *Speculum* 86, no. 1 (January 2011): 42–78.

Witzel, H.J. "Der geographische Exkurs in den lateinischen Geschichtequellen des Mittelalters." PhD diss., Univ. of Frankfurt am Main, 1952.

Witzel, H.J. "Le problème de l'auteur des *Gesta Francorum et aliorum Hierosolimitanorum*." Translated by F. Vercauteren. *Le Moyen Age* 61 (1955): 319–28.

Wright, Roger. *Late Latin and Early Romance in Spain and Carolingian France*. Liverpool, 1982.

Wyke, Maria. *Caesar: A Life in Western Culture*. Chicago, 2007.

Name Index

Achillas, 100
Adalbert of Metz, Duke, 9
Adèle of Champagne, 72–3, 130n7
Aeneas, 19, 83–4
Agnes, daughter of Boniface de Montferrat, 41
Aimoinus of Fleury, 132n27
Aleaumes de Clari, 57–8, 127n13
Alexander, 97, 127n10
Alexius I (emperor of Constantinople), 117n2, 117n3, 118n4, 120n29, 121n32, 123–4n20, 127n13
Alexius III (emperor of Constantinople), 51–3, 124n20
Alexius IV (emperor of Constantinople), 63–6, 66
Ambiorix, 75–6
Andronicus, 66–7, 127–8n13
Angilbert, 11, 16–17, 115n3, 117n20
Anna Comnena, 29, 120n31
Ansols de Rémi, 42, 59
Antonius, 78
Arnulfus, 130n11, 134n4
Arsenoe, 100
Augustine, Saint, xii, 77
Aurelia, 79–80

Baldwin (count of Flanders and Hainaut), 55, 58, 125n22, 125n23, 130n7
Baldwin, John, 129n2
Baldwin, M.W., 119n22
Baldwin of Boulogne, 26–7, 118n3, 120n29, 120n30
Bancourt, Paul, 121n37
Baudri de Bourgeuil, x, 21, 24, 113n4, 119n12, 119n19
Baudri de Deuil. *See* Baudri de Bourgeuil
Bautier, Robert-Henri, 129n4, 129n5
Becker, Alfons, 119n22
Beer, Jeanette, 114n14, 116n10, 122n6, 123n18, 130n16, 131n19, 134n35 (chap. 5), 134n6 (chap. 6)
Bernard of Septimania, 9
Berosus, 100
Berthe, 115n3
Blake, E.O., 118n5
Boccaccio, 132n27
Bohemond, x, 19–22, 27–31, 33, 36, 117n1, 117n2, 117n3, 120n28, 120–1n32, 122n42

Subject Index

abbé de Vaux, 53, 125n22
Abbéville Gospels, 15
abbreviation, 43–4, 47, 59, 80, 92–5
ablative absolute, 26
absolution, 48–9
adjective, 5, 26–8, 32–3, 41–2, 50
Adrianople, 40, 41, 55, 57
Aduatuci, 98, 134n5
adverb, 10, 14, 26–8, 32–3
Aedui, 88, 133n33
Aeneid, 83–4, 106
Aix, 8
Aleppo, 34
Aler, L', 85
Alexandria, 64–5, 100, 131–2n26
Alexandri Magni iter ad Paradisum, 77
Alexiad, 29, 120n31
aliquantulum, xiii, 20–1
alliteration, 6, 32, 53, 83
allusion, xi, xiv, 25, 32, 50, 54–5, 61
Amalfi, 19, 21
Amazon, 33
Amiens, 57
amplification, 29–30, 35, 53, 78,
     99–102, 131n22
anachronism, x, 3, 15, 17, 30–1, 35–6,
     53–4, 56, 104–5, 117n2, 130n16,
     134n9

Analogies, 85
anaphora, 52
Angevin, 72
Annales (Flodoard), 110
Annales regni francorum, 117n19
annominatio, 50, 53
Anti-Cato, 85
Antioch, 19–22, 25, 27, 28–30, 33,
     35–6, 106, 117n1, 118n3, 118n4,
     120n28, 121n32, 122n42
antiquity, ix, xi–xiii, xiv, 45, 79, 84–5,
     91, 104
antithesis, 50, 53, 123n18
aphorism, 79–80, 83
apology, 4, 58–9, 105
apostrophe, 27–8, 50, 53, 96–8,
     123n18
Apulia, x, 21–2, 33–4, 117n1
Aquitaine, 8
Argentaria. *See* Strasbourg
Arras, 72–3
Artois, 72–3
Ascalon, x, 19, 35, 106
assumption, 34, 59, 74, 104–6,
     114n14
athlete for Christ, 30
auctor, 45, 74, 77–90, 91–6, 114n10,
     115n17 (foreword), 115n6 (chap. 1)